Reinventing English

Reinventing English

Teaching in the Contact Zone

John
Gaughan

Boynton/Cook Publishers
HEINEMANN
Portsmouth, NH

Boynton/Cook Publishers, Inc.
A subsidiary of Reed Elsevier Inc.
361 Hanover Street
Portsmouth, NH 03801–3912
www.boyntoncook.com

Offices and agents throughout the world

The author and publisher wish to thank those who have generously given permission to reprint borrowed material:

"From Comfort Zone to Contact Zone" by John Gaughan was first published in *English Journal,* Volume 87, Number 2. Excerpts reprinted by permission of the National Council of Teachers of English.

"Making Our Mark: Defining 'Self' in a Multicultural World" by John Gaughan was first published in *Voices from the Middle,* Volume 6, Number 3. Excerpts reprinted by permission of the National Council of Teachers of English.

The poems "Mama" and "History / Herstory" by Mary Pierce Brosmer are reprinted by permission of the poet.

"From Literature to Language: Personal Writing and Critical Pedagogy" by John Gaughan was first published in *English Education,* Volume 31, Number 4. Excerpts reprinted by permission of the National Council of Teachers of English.

"Cincinnati" from *Camp Notes and Other Writings* by Mitsuye Yamada. Copyright © 1992 by Mitsuye Yamada. Reprinted by permission of Rutgers University Press.

Library of Congress Cataloging-in-Publication Data
Gaughan, John
    Reinventing English : teaching in the contact zone / John Gaughan.
        p.   cm.
    Includes bibliographical references.
    ISBN 0-86709-501-6
    1. English language—Study and teaching (Secondary)—Social aspects—
United States.   2. Language arts (Secondary)—Social aspects—United States.
I. Title: Teaching in the contact zone.   II. Title.

    LB1631 .G245   2001
    428'.0071'273—dc21
                                                                    00-050764

Editor: William Varner
Production service: Lisa Garboski, bookworks
Production coordinator: Elizabeth Valway
Cover design: Joni Doherty Design
Manufacturing: Louise Richardson

Printed in the United States of America on acid-free paper
05   04   03   02   01   DA   1   2   3   4   5

Dedicated to Tom Romano,
who entered my life as a mentor,
worked with me as a colleague,
became a source of inspiration, and
remains forever my friend.

Contents

Acknowledgments   xi

1   **From Comfort Zone to Contact Zone**   1

2   **Challenging Assumptions/
    Shaping Identity**   2

   TEACHING STRATEGIES
   - *Questions to prompt critical thinking*
   - *Generating metaphors*
   - *Picture books to prompt writing*
   - *Using multiple genres to write about place*
   - *Diaries as models*
   - *Mimicking voices*
   - *Round-robin responding*
   - *Student writing to spark discussion*

3   **Prejudice—A Case Study**   31

   TEACHING STRATEGIES
   - *Brainstorming stereotypes*
   - *Challenging assumptions*
   - *Prompting rethinking*
   - *Four Corners*
   - *Teacher modeling*
   - *Extending conversations*
   - *Rethinking through portfolios*

4 Cultural Representation 45

TEACHING STRATEGIES

- *Brainstorming cultural images*
- *Juxtaposing cultural texts*
- *Immersion in cultural themes*
- *Imagination and cultural reflection*

5 Silence and Sexism 56

TEACHING STRATEGIES

- *Four Corners*
- *Brainstorming myths*
- *Stereotypes and poetry*
- *Reading and writing personal ads*
- *Learning centers*
- *Putting characters on trial*

6 War and Voice—Speaking Up 82

TEACHING STRATEGIES

- *Centers and complicity*
- *Writing about reading*
- *Writing about film and literature*
- *Imagining other perspectives*
- *Rereading and rethinking*
- *Poems in two voices*
- *Reflecting through talk shows*

7 Sex and Sexuality 107

TEACHING STRATEGIES

- *Surveying students*
- *Elaborating responses*
- *A questionnaire*
- *Literature circles*
- *Responding to student writing*
- *Final reflections*

8 Censorship and Faith 123

TEACHING STRATEGIES
- *Defending texts*
- *Considering texts*
- *Constructing a defense*

9 Contact and Context 133

Works Cited 139

Acknowledgments

In 1995 Tom Romano returned to Ohio after teaching for four years at Utah State in Logan, Utah. I was glad to have him back. From the time I student-taught with Tom in 1982, he's been a constant source of encouragement. He urged me to attend the Ohio Writing Project. He invited me to present with him at NCTE. He suggested I try to publish my work. Now he was back, teaching a graduate class at Miami University called The Teaching of Writing. In his class I wrote a case study that was published in *Teacher Research;* a chapter for my first book; and a multigenre paper that became the first such article published in *English Journal.* I also outlined a prospectus for this book in my final portfolio for his class. In no course I've ever taken have I managed to be so productive. Yes, I was glad Tom was back. I owe my teaching career and professional life to his inspiration.

Tom introduced me to Mary Pierce Brosmer (to whom I'll introduce you in Chapter 5). Mary attended the Writing Project two years before me and became my instructor when I enrolled in a follow-up course she taught several years later. Like Tom, Mary knows how to inspire and encourage, how to help her students and colleagues find their voices. She's helped me and I want to publicly thank her.

My friends and colleagues Renee Dickson, Katie Charles, Linda Tatman, and Jennifer Drake worked with me on a series of vignettes about the contact zone that we were invited to present locally and at NCTE. Talking with them about their experiences in the contact zone helped me to rethink my own. Thanks for sharing your teaching.

I'd like to thank Tom Gaffigan, Amy Wilson, Sara Boose, Leah Howard, Jenn Johnson, Patti (Osborn) O'Malley, and Donnie Becker, who all student-taught with me at some point during the writing of this book. Their influence helped shaped my vision of what English can be and how it might be taught in the high school classroom.

I want to thank Mary Ehrenworth for reading a first draft of this manuscript and Bill Varner, my editor, for working so patiently with me, especially in the latter stages of revisions.

My wife, Kathy, and my daughters, Amy and Kelly, gave me long periods of uninterrupted time to work on the book, and I want to give them my sincere thanks.

Finally, I want to thank my students, who shared their writing, their feelings, and their attitudes, helping me reconsider what teaching is all about. I thank them for permitting me to include their work here.

From Comfort Zone
to Contact Zone

Cliff

Cliff files past my desk, unwraps his bulky blue Starter jacket, and slumps into a seat near the rear window. His dark sweatshirt hoods his head, and when his chin sinks to his folded hands, I barely see his eyes.

Cliff's father died several months ago when his truck spun out of control on an icy interstate south of Cincinnati known as the cut in the hill. He was only 35. I never saw his son grieve. Cliff missed several days of school around the funeral, but when he returned, it was as if nothing had happened . . . except Cliff craved attention even more than he had before. Any attention.

Last week he smuggled Mountain Dew into class for him and two buddies; the week before he littered the floor under his desk with empty Starburst wrappers. I wondered what Cliff was up to today when I noticed his head bobbing as if he were watching a concert. Then I heard the tinny sound of Walkman music and understood Cliff's hood.

"Hand it over," I said. "You can have it back after class."

"It's Seven Mary Three. Let me at least finish the song."

"Now, Cliff."

Later that period, while conferring with Shelly, I caught him pelting a peer across the room with modeling clay. Apparently, they'd been volleying for several minutes.

"See me after class, Cliff."

"What, are ya crazy? I didn't throw anything. Danny's been throwing it at me."

"See me after class, Cliff and Danny."

"I ain't seein' nobody," Cliff argued.

As I wrote out the detentions, Cliff gathered his coat and stomped out the door.

Class Discussion Following the Film *Casualties of War*

Shelly: I can't believe Sergeant Meserve ordered his men to kidnap that girl.

Nikki: They did more than kidnap her. They raped her.

Cliff: It was war. War is war.

Danielle: You're not saying it's okay to rape just because it's war?

Cliff: I'm saying there're different rules in wartime.

Nikki: They didn't have to go along with their sergeant. Erikson didn't.

Mike: Yeah, but you're supposed to follow orders.

Cliff: You tell 'em. They were hard up. What soldier isn't? And besides, she probably wanted it. (He winks at Mike as he says this.)

Shelly (raising her voice): I can't believe you said that.

Me: Hold on, hold on. Cliff, do you think soldiers should follow any order they're given, even if they think it's wrong?

Cliff: You have to follow orders in the army. You can't have each soldier deciding whether an order's right or not. They'd all be dead.

Me: But whose life was threatened in this situation? They kidnapped her at night. She hadn't done any harm to them.

Cliff: The gooks had just killed his best friend. He was getting revenge. Besides, my uncle fought in Vietnam, and he said you couldn't trust anyone—old people, women, kids—no one.

Me: So rape is justifiable in war?

Cliff: Sometimes.

Marcia

Marcia has taken five classes from me and passed two. Each semester she passed she missed only fifteen days. Usually her absences number forty or more. Whether it's a bum knee or strep throat, Marcia finds some reason to skip school. When she returns, a scribbled excuse from her mother accompanies her. I've never seen her father.

Five weeks into the quarter, I call her parents.

"Mrs. Sheffield, Marcia's failing English."

"Oh, yeah, I know, she's been so sick, can't shake that darn infection; we've had her at the doctor's, but they can't figure it out; she's been on three different antibiotics, but say, Marcia's been tellin' me 'bout that book she's readin' . . . "

"*The Drowning of Stephan Jones?*" I say.

"Yeah, that's the one. Ya know there's a lot of bad stuff in that book. Do ya think the kids need to be readin' about all that violence?"

"It happens, Mrs. Sheffield. I want students to think about different kinds of discrimination."

"But we teach Marcia homosexuality's wrong. I mean I can't tell people how to live their life, if they want to live in sin, but . . . "

"Listen, Mrs. Sheffield," I interrupt, "I just wanted you to be aware that Marcia's failing. She needs to be in school to pass. We can talk about this book later if you'll call me at the end of the day. I have to go to my next class now. Can someone pick up Marcia's work for her?"

"Sure thing, but . . ."

"It's been nice talking to you. Goodbye."

Marcia's self-conscious about her body. She wears a powder-blue down coat—grimy with industrial grit and car exhaust—even in warm weather. Her glasses are thick, her black hair unkempt, her skin pockmarked and pimpled. When she does attend school, she sits by herself. No one ever wants to pair up with her or work in her peer group. When called on to answer a question, she blurts out responses that bring giggles from classmates and redden her face. No wonder she misses so much school.

Letter from Mr. Sheffield

Dear Mr. Gaughan:

Due to objections we have with the novel you assigned our daughter Marcia, we are requesting she be removed from your class. As Christians we accept the Bible as the inspired word of God and believe its condemnation of homosexuality is correct (Leviticus 18:22-30 and Romans 1:24-28).

We believe the body is the temple of the Lord and should not be abused. Taking drugs, smoking cigarettes, starving oneself, and overeating affect only the abuser. Sexual promiscuity, including homosexuality, threaten the innocent.

We believe God created man with the ability to make choices and then accept the consequences, good or bad. Whether you like it or not, homosexuality is a choice. Liberals like yourself are attempting to deodorize it and make society the scapegoat.

If you were dealing with the Truth concerning controversial subjects and not just the wishful thinking of confused minds, we wouldn't be writing this letter.

Again, we are requesting that the counselor get Marcia out of this course and never place her in your class again.

Sincerely,
Marvin Sheffield

Lorraine

Lorraine is one of the most cynical students I've taught, but her cynicism doesn't make her pasty-face-white, head-to-toe-black gloomy like other students I've known. She's never written suicide letters or poetry bemoaning the absurdity of the universe.

I'd call Lorraine a pragmatic cynic. She's a matter-of-fact, tell-it-like-she-sees-it kind of girl. I enjoy having her in class. Once or twice a period I can count on her to share her thoughts, not in a class-clown, look-at-me sort of way, but thoughtfully, even sensitively. Lorraine is a tactful cynic, too.

She usually directs her barbs at figures outside the class, more often outside the school. Sometimes the principal, more likely the president. Her comments make us laugh.

Lorraine and Kathy are best friends, both five-feet-two, with short hair and bright eyes. Each day they enter class like twins, laughing (at whom I always wonder), heavy backpacks slung across their shoulders, continuing a conversation they'd begun at lunch. So animated is their discussion, you wish their energy were contagious and you'd lunched with them so you, too, were in the know.

Despite her cynical attitude, Lorraine's writing can be sensitive, as in a recent vignette about her grandfather, which begins, "I remember you heard me praying . . . 'Dear Lord, protect my family and the ones who protect me, especially my grandpapa.'"

A sentimental cynic, that Lorraine.

Excerpt from Lorrain's
Paper "Keep It To Myself"

Leaving the mall I walk steadily to my car. I silently watch everything around me.

It's black. My keys are ready to go into the lock.

Walk quickly.

Get in.

Slam door shut.

Lock it.

Start engine.

Whenever someone is attacked, robbed, raped, or killed, I see a black man doing it. Why? I'm not a racist. I'm Southern, by God. (Okay, bad excuse.) I'm not really sure why I feel this way. It wasn't how I was raised, I know that much.

I keep it to myself. Don't let anyone know how I really feel.

I would like to tell all their lazy, no good, shootin' each other, drug sellin', Dairy Mart workin', cop killin', pimpin' ain't easy, jewelry stealin', walkin' up on Fountain Square tryin' to sell me some perfume, welfare dependin', tax cheatin', havin' more kids than they have names for to get more money, organized drive by shootin', car stealin', house burnin', girlfriend beatin', lootin' from their own store, gangster riotin', rag wearin' asses to quit complaining and get back to work. You owe us Republicans some money.

Beginning at the End

Injustice anywhere is a threat to justice everywhere.

—Martin Luther King (1963)

Never doubt that a small group of thoughtful committed citizens can change the world; in fact it is the only thing that ever does.

—Margaret Mead (1996)

A week before I started teaching my first class in 1982, my principal handed me the newly revised curriculum, collated, divided, and hole-punched, collected in a thick green binder. "Your bible," he told me. "Just follow it and keep things under control." Bound by objectives and rigid assessments, I dutifully directed students toward each test of basic skills, hoping for mastery. No matter that Kristy was frustrated because she hadn't mastered the participle test in five attempts; she was bound by the curriculum and so was I. She'd have to keep trying. Or that Doug had trouble with vocabulary words such as *dichotomy* and *schism*. Our curriculum was the tie that binds.

Although the curriculum troubled me, I have to admit that it was, in some ways, comfortable. Teach to the objectives, assign the chapter questions, administer the pre-fab tests, and move on. I never heard then that "rape is permissible," that "gays live in sin," or that "blacks commit all the crimes." The curriculum was too controlled for that. None of my students were nudged out of their comfort zone. They may have been frustrated by skills they couldn't master, but because this pattern of teaching and learning resembled what school had always been for them, they were at least comfortable in their frustration.

But I wasn't. This curriculum didn't make sense to me. I began to ask myself: What is English? What is it for? What should English teachers be trying to accomplish? What content should we be teaching?

In *The Challenge to Care in Schools: An Alternative Approach to Education*, Nel Noddings quotes Mortimer Adler and Robert Maynard Hutchins: Adler says that, "All children . . . should have exactly the same education at least through high school," agreeing with Hutchins that, "The best education for the best is the best education for all" (Noddings 1992, 163). Although this sounds fair and democratic, is an identical education really the best for all students?

Noddings questions not only the education offered to those considered the "best"; she questions America's "best" themselves:

> Are the persons who have governed, produced acknowledged works of art, built fortunes, and conducted military campaigns really our best persons? Did their education produce a goodness we really want to replicate, or has its acquisition merely been the defining mark of those who claimed themselves to be the best? If a different sort of education had been offered, might our best have been a more compassionate, more generous, more open, less judgmental, less acquisitive, and wiser set of persons? (164)

In *Reshaping High School English* Bruce Pirie echoes Noddings' questions with questions of his own: "Are we Warriors in a Crusade of High Culture? If so, why? Would that be because we believe that kind of Culture makes people superior moral beings? How then do we handle the inconvenient fact that the Nazi commanders in World War II were notorious connoisseurs of culture?" (Pirie 1997, 22)

These questions prompted me to return to the beginning, to what I do know about English: it is a language, so we should *immerse* students in it as we would the study of any language—they should speak it, listen to it, read it, and write it. They should learn to express themselves clearly—orally and in writing. They should become familiar with writers who use the language well in a variety of genres. They should experiment with their own language use. But what bearing does that immersion have on the curricular content?

In his memoir *'Tis* Frank McCourt challenged the curricular content he encountered in New York City public schools:

> I couldn't let days dribble by in the routine of high school grammar, spelling, vocabulary, digging for the deeper meaning in poetry, bits of literature doled out for the multiple choice tests that would follow so that universities can be supplied with the best and the brightest. I had to begin to enjoy the act of teaching and the only way I could do that was start over, teach what I loved and to hell with the curriculum (McCourt 1999, 340).

Should English teachers follow McCourt's advice and just teach what they love? Or should something besides personal interests and tastes guide us? Ben Nelms says, "We need to reinvent English" (Nelms 1994, 104–5). If that is so, what should the "reinvention" look like?

Consider these headlines:

Jewish Center Victim Still in Hospital

23 Women Killed in the Name of Love

Murder Charges Planned in Beating Death of Gay Student

Racism to Be Key Issue in Third Dragging-Death Trial

Dozens of similar ones could be culled from newspapers around the country every day. Whether the hate arose because of religion, gender, sexual orientation, or race, the end results are the same—beatings, abuse, and murder. Unfortunately, schools mirror society:

- West Paducah, Kentucky: 3 students killed and 5 wounded
- Jonesboro, Arkansas: 4 students and 1 teacher killed, 10 others wounded
- Springfield, Oregon: 2 students killed and 22 others wounded
- Littleton, Colorado: 14 students and 1 teacher killed, 23 others wounded

Perhaps Nel Noddings' advice can guide our reinvention of curriculum: "What children need to learn is how to sympathize and empathize with other people and to understand their own inclinations toward cruelty and violence" (Noddings 1992, 55).

To begin to understand these inclinations, students need to examine where they are and where they're coming from. "Only when the given or the taken-for-granted is subject to questioning, only when we take various, sometimes unfamiliar perspectives on it, does it show itself as what it is" (Greene 1995, 23).

The headlines and school shootings shed a different light on the traditional curriculum. Hate crimes are on the rise, and the perpetrators are coming in younger shapes and sizes. The gun"man" near Flint, Michigan, who shot his five-year-old classmate was only six years old himself. The gun"men" in Jonesboro, Arkansas, were eleven and thirteen. The shooter in West Paducah, Kentucky, was fourteen.

Eric Harris, eighteen, from Littleton, Colorado, explains his motivation for killing (and no doubt the motivation that inspired other school shootings) in the suicide note (Vaughan) he left behind:

> Your children who have ridiculed me, who have chosen not to accept me, who have treated me like I am not worth their time, are dead.

THEY ARE (expletive) DEAD . . . . Surely you will try to blame it on
the clothes I wear, the music I listen to, or the way I choose to present
myself, but no. Do not hide behind my choices. You need to face the
fact that this comes as a result of YOUR CHOICES.

    Parents and teachers, you f—— up. You have taught these kids
to not accept what is different. YOU ARE IN THE WRONG. I have
taken their lives and my own but it was your doing. Teachers, parents,
LET THIS MASSACRE BE ON YOUR SHOULDERS UNTIL THE DAY
YOU DIE.

Harris's note makes me squirm. He was sick, he was ruthless, he
was a murderer. His note doesn't justify his actions. Still, it makes me
squirm. How well *have* we taught our children to accept difference? Not
just to tolerate it, but to embrace it? How often *do* we overlook cruelty
in our neighborhoods and classrooms and rationalize that kids will be
kids? Do we really believe that sticks and stones will break our children's bones but names will never hurt them?

The "jocks" at Columbine High School didn't deserve to die. Students who are different don't deserve humiliation either. The social
pecking order in American high schools mirrors our societal pecking
order, and if we don't do something to stop it, more students will die in
school and more citizens will die in America.

Whether we like it or not, schools must address societal problems.
Teachers may not have gone to college to become counselors or psy-
chologists, but sometimes we must play those roles. Given the climate
in schools today, if we don't address these problems, critics will consider
us negligent. They may be right. Teachers at Columbine were criticized
for ignoring a "death video" Harris and Klebold made for a class presentation and for ignoring other signs that something was wrong (*Cincinnati Enquirer*, 23 April 1999, A2/letter to the editor; *USA Today*, 23 April
1999, 14A).

I'm not arguing for a curriculum that has as its goal detecting problem students (although that might be a by-product); instead, I'd like
to see us address student problems. "The traditional organization of
schooling is intellectually and morally inadequate for contemporary
society. We live in an age troubled by social problems that force us to
reconsider what we do in schools" (Noddings 1992, 173). What we do
and how we do it are still key questions, but why we do what we do is
most significant.

Throughout this book I will discuss reading and writing methods
that have worked in my classes, but more importantly, I will suggest a
different content and different end for English education. Exposing students to the British and American canons; having them write academic
analyses of their reading; and acquainting them with different literary
periods was, at one time, the job of high school English teachers, espe-

cially considering that preparing students to read and write at the college level was a primary goal. Today, I think that goal is secondary.

I still believe teachers should prepare students for postsecondary education, but we should prepare them first for life. Preparing them for college should not preclude appreciating difference. Reading contemporary and young-adult literature about people different from themselves, thinking critically about it, and expressing that thinking in writing *will* prepare them for college and, at the same time, help them empathize with people of different races, religions, and sexual orientation.

I say help them empathize because resistance often precedes empathy. Sometimes students' first response to difference is fear, fear borne out of ignorance. Rather than admit fear, though, students resist. "I'm not reading a book about fags" is a common reaction from homophobic students when we begin a unit about discrimination toward gays. That homophobia is not usually grounded in experience. In fact, most of my students who voice such objections have never actually met a gay person, at least not to their knowledge. If there's any hope that such students might become empathetic, they need to get to know someone who's gay, if not in actuality, then through literature.

Statements such as the one above, grounded in values that oppose those of their teacher, epitomize a place known as the contact zone, "where cultures meet, clash, and grapple with each other . . ."(Pratt 1991). *Reinventing English* is about the clashing and grappling my students and I have done when we meet in the contact zone of the classroom. It is about opening minds to difference. That doesn't mean I expect students to reject their religious faith or doubt their sexual orientation. I do hope, though, they will be willing to think about people who don't believe the same things or live the same lives that they do. This process takes time. I will share how I engage students in that process through the various thematic units I teach at Lockland High School.

In Chapter 2, "Challenging Assumptions/Shaping Identity," students explore the assumptions that underlie their thinking, especially how *place* and *family* shape identity, and how their identities evolve as they discuss with their peers such issues as ethics and immigration.

The racial prejudices that reveal themselves at the end of Chapter 2 are explored further in Chapter 3, "Prejudice—A Case Study." Misty, whose writing usually expressed a great deal of empathy, revealed her bias toward Latinos in a new piece because of an incident that had occurred the summer before. Through conferences, class work, and her own writing process, Misty rethinks her prejudices in this chapter, the case history of one student working in the contact zone.

All of us are hyphenated Americans. If we hope to live in harmony in the twenty-first century, we need to listen to the voices of others.

One way to enhance our understanding of other races and cultures is to read literature or watch films about people different from us. But what if those books or movies misrepresent a culture or perpetuate misunderstandings? Does it matter who writes the story, directs the film, or plays the role? In Chapter 4, "Cultural Representation," I describe a unit a former student teacher and I taught in which we discuss these issues and show teachers how to engage students in this debate.

Students are often unaware of their own prejudices, especially in relation to gender. In Chapter 5, "Silence and Sexism," I show readers how I organize a class called Women and Men by focusing on silence first and moving students to voice. Once they break the silence, they consider how language can lead to discrimination, harassment, and assault. I share texts and assignments that help students consider gender differences and their own sexist attitudes in ways they never have before.

In Chapter 6, "War and Voice—Speaking Up," I outline a course I teach about the Holocaust, in which students explore the perspective of victims and perpetrators through texts such as *Night* and *Triumph of the Spirit* and then of "innocent" bystanders through *Obedience* and *The Wave*. Students are encouraged to connect the past and present by exploring their own experiences with discrimination and to consider silence and complicity in the face of cruelty and evil.

Chapter 7, "Sex and Sexuality," grew out of a homophobic response I include at the end of the previous chapter. It revolves around a unit that asks students to consider sexuality through surveys, novels, short stories, and their own writing. Changing their angle of vision helps them understand perspectives and empathize with others who may or may not be different from them.

Chapter 8, "Censorship and Faith," is a bit misleading in that when most people think of school censorship, they think of community members challenging books. This chapter, though, is about a text I debated using and the complications that followed when a student's faith forced me to reconsider what is appropriate in the classroom.

In Chapter 9, "Contact and Context," I reiterate the importance of establishing contexts that will help students think critically about the origin of their prejudices and to reconsider their assumptions about others.

Besides sharing teaching strategies throughout the book, I refer to and summarize examples of the contemporary, multicultural texts students read and watch and the thematic contexts in which I use them.

*   *   *

Fifty years ago the classroom in which I currently teach did not exist as it does now. The physical space was present, but the student population was segregated. Thoughtful, committed citizens like Martin Luther King have since addressed the injustices created by a segregated America. Because of those citizens, Chaunisha and Chuck now learn side by side.

Reinventing English is about creating opportunities for students to become thoughtful, committed citizens. It is about encouraging them to air their views honestly and forthrightly. Those views don't exist in a vacuum, though, and students need to realize that. They need to explore the assumptions that underlie their opinions and consider how those opinions relate to their peers, their community, and their country.

Essentially, this book is about social justice and thematic teaching. Out of that teaching, texts evolve that shake me from my comfort zone: Cliff's response that "rape is permissible in wartime"; Marvin Sheffield's letter condemning homosexuality; Lorraine's beliefs that she'd previously "kept to herself." These revelations aren't as simple to address as identifying past and present participles.

I want Cliff to consider where Private Erikson in *Casualties of War* and the soldiers who resisted Lt. Calley at My Lai are coming from, but I want to keep Cliff talking, too. I want Mr. Sheffield to admit that teaching a book about discrimination toward gays is legitimate for my Contemporary Culture class. I want Lorraine to reconsider her waterfall of racist thoughts, but I want to keep her writing honestly.

These meetings in the contact zone make me reconsider what and how I teach. I hope they challenge you to reconsider your own teaching—not only the methods you use but the ends to which you teach. When Ben Nelms said that, "We need to reinvent English," he added, "No glib redefinition or timid reform effort will do" (Nelms 1994, 104–5). I hope you find this effort neither timid nor glib. I hope its end of creating thoughtful, committed citizens is one worthy enough for you to consider reform attempts of your own.

2

Challenging Assumptions/ Shaping Identity

TEACHING STRATEGIES
- *Questions to prompt critical thinking*
- *Generating metaphors*
- *Picture books to prompt writing*
- *Using multiple genres to write about place*
- *Diaries as models*
- *Mimicking voices*
- *Round-robin responding*
- *Student writing to spark discussion*

"Immigration sucks."

Billy

"My writing sucks."

Billy

"Who are you?"

Pete Townsend (1983)

Assumptions and Identity

We spend our whole lives trying to answer this question sung by The Who in the 1970s. Billy is trying to answer it now. Thinking about where he lives, his relationship to family and friends, his popularity in school, his social position as an American citizen, Billy struggles to understand and shape his identity. On the outside he's six feet tall and husky, with brown eyes, closely cropped hair, and a perpetual smile. Billy plays football. He's a fifth-year senior who envisions a future in the Marines. He's polite to his teachers, although he doesn't like school. He freely admits loving his mother, whom he calls his best friend. Not everyone is his friend, though. Billy is a bigot.

English teachers have a chance to help students formulate answers to the question Who are you? By structuring our classes so students feel free to express who they are (at least at that moment) and by discussing topics that mirror their teenage interests, students will use our classroom to try on their emerging identities. Once they've become acclimated to high school English, I encourage them to reflect upon who they see themselves becoming.

I begin with a series of questions:

- Do you celebrate Christmas at home or with relatives?
- Do any of you girls carry tissues in your purses?
- Which college will you attend?
- Why do people in England drive on the wrong side of the road?
- Have any of you guys ever been asked to carry cases of pop?
- Did you hear Eddie Fingers this morning on EBN?
- Will you girls take your husband's name when you marry?

I'm not particularly interested in students' answers to these questions, but I do want them to consider the assumptions that underlie each one. Some students aren't Christian and don't celebrate Christmas. Guys may carry Kleenex; girls may not. Many students can't afford college or have no desire to continue their education. The side of the road one drives on is arbitrary—not right or wrong, but right or left. Girls can carry cases of pop, though in our school they're rarely asked to do so. Some girls will never marry and may not be interested in the opposite sex. Most of my students don't listen to white rock'n'roll.

We don't know who we are without examining some of the assumptions that underlie our lives. These questions quickly make that apparent. Various positions affect our identity. Gender, birth order, nationality, religion, race, school, family, and sexuality are just a few.

Since names and identity are so intertwined (see Gaughan, *Cultural Reflections* (1997)), I ask students to consider metaphors that reflect identity: skater, grit, yuppie, pozer, skinhead, homeboy, jock, headbanger (Pugh et al. 1992, 33). They write about what each metaphor means to them and with which metaphor(s) they identify. Misty adds some to her list: hoe (sleeps around, wears sleazy clothes); player (goes out with more than one girl at a time); wigger (tries to act black); perpetrator (spreads rumors); and sellout (forgets where he/she comes from). This last one proves a springboard to our first piece of writing.

Place and Identity

I want students to think about the relationship of place to identity. I read them aloud the children's book *Life in the Ghetto,* showing them the pictures along the way (Thomas 1991). The author, Anika D. Thomas, was thirteen when she wrote and illustrated this story about growing up in the Hill District north of Pittsburgh. Through her story she discusses respect, apathy, behavior, family, hope, community, and identity. When we finish reading, I ask my students to write a similar piece called "Life in Lockland" or "Life in Arlington." (Arlington is the small community adjacent to Lockland from which many of our students come.) I tell them to list the topics Thomas discusses—respect, apathy, etc.—and to brainstorm incidents from their own lives that relate to each one. They can invent their own related topics as well. When they're done brainstorming, they pair up and exchange lists with a partner who questions them about anything on their list. Students share stories, ask additional questions, and fill in details, all the while rehearsing their writing before they actually draft.

I was surprised the first time I asked students to complete this assignment. I didn't expect the gloomy tone. Dae Dae begins her paper:

> The West Side of Lockland would be the perfect place for a "gangsta" movie. You have your drunks, drug dealers and users, bad kids running around cursing, . . . breaking into car windows, . . . breaking into stores. You can have all of the above happening on my street alone. I live on Elm Street. This is the last street in Lockland before entering Wyoming. I live the real-life nightmare on Elm Street.
>
> Walking home is like entering a totally different environment. Near the school you have the pretty houses with porches and flowers planted all around the yard. You have the pale-faced children chasing each other, laughing and playing . . .
>
> I cross Wayne Avenue and it's like crossing the New York State line. . . . Still I walk further down the street. Further down the drain until I empty out into my home.

Dae Dae's paper continues in this vein, vividly describing the disintegration around her until this bit of salvation:

> At the end of Walnut is Elm Street. My house is protected from the drunks and druggies by the beautiful flowers and the wire garden fence. Like a small island lost at sea. I smell the sweet fragrance of the roses as I cross the street. The sun is brightly shining in my face as I walk to our back yard. I sit my book bag down and look out front. We truly live as though we are the family in a bubble. My mom tells me to always keep to myself. She says the trash belongs with the other trash. . . . As though no one in Lockland has any morals and just runs wild. . . . I guess my family are the only humans in the bunch.

Dae Dae rarely spoke in my class. She stutters, especially when she's nervous. She traces her stuttering to an incident in grade school when a teacher criticized her response to a question. School's been a struggle ever since. She's always worn dresses or skirts to school, never pants. Her peers pick on her because of her clothes. Dae Dae told me her mother is religious, that she wasn't permitted to wear pants to school. Looking after younger siblings adversely affected her attendance junior year. I wondered if she'd ever make it. Senior year she got pregnant, but despite one more obstacle, she found a way to graduate. I know she'll try to protect her child as her mother tries to protect her, to fence off her own island, to retain her humanity.

Dae Dae may stutter when she speaks, but her writing never stutters. She finds herself in this piece about Lockland and makes meaning by comparing the pretty houses and pale children near school to the "trash" on Elm Street, flowers linking both worlds. I'm still overwhelmed by the depressing details of Dae Dae's life but encouraged by her conclusion and its glimmer of hope.

Little hope is reflected, though, in Billy's "Life in Arlington Heights" paper:

> We moved into one of the shittiest apartments in Arlington Heights. When I first started to move, I thought that I was going to cry. It was an old apartment building with dead bushes around the driveway. As soon as I opened the door to go into the building, the nastiest stench struck my nostrils like Evander Holyfield hitting Mike Tyson. It smelled like old, rotten milk. I thought I was going to puke. . . .
>
> When I walked in the apartment, my mother was talking to a neighbor who I know had to weigh about four hundred pounds. Her name was Ruthie. I had never met anyone that big in person. I said Hi. My mother introduced me. Her arms were as thick as my thighs. It was sick. She sat there smoking cigarettes and drinking a diet Coke. I think she needs to do a little more than just drink diet Coke. This woman needs some liposuction or something. Later that day I saw her getting into her 1976 Dodge. I thought the shocks on the driver side

weren't going to hold. I'm surprised that the driver side didn't scrape when she drove down the road. . . .

I hope I won't live around here very long. It might drive me insane.

Billy's piece is problematic. I'm glad he wrote it. It helps me understand where he's coming from. His parents had gotten divorced. His mom was trying to support him and his sister. Their new apartment had only two bedrooms, so they took turns sleeping on the couch. His living conditions are less than plush. But Billy's own prejudices continue to reveal themselves. His passages about the apartment and Ruthie are descriptive. He experiments with metaphorical writing, but the content of that metaphor is racist—that black people smell. The familiar *sucks* continues to populate his language and his emerging identity. No one wants to "suck." But if everything around you "sucks" (at least, as you perceive those things), it is difficult to find the flowers of hope that Dae Dae does as she reflects on her life. Billy isn't there yet. I was bothered by the racist remarks in his paper, but I thought it too early in the semester to comment upon them. At this point, I wanted to keep students writing so that they still might examine different perspectives.

Multiple Genres

One way to make the familiarity of place unfamiliar is to have students explore a topic through multiple genres. *Our America: Life and Death on the South Side of Chicago* is an appropriate introduction to this kind of writing, because the authors use dialogs, anecdotes, interviews, and character sketches to paint a picture of life in their neighborhood (Jones and Newman 1997). Written by LeAlan Jones and Lloyd Newman, two teenagers from South Chicago, the book recounts stories of growing up under difficult circumstances. The grimmest story the authors relate is the murder of a five-year-old boy who was dropped from the window of a building near their homes. Although the conditions are harsh in the Ida B. Wells housing project, the book is uplifting. As LeAlan puts it: "We have a hard life, but we're sensitive. Ghetto kids are not a different breed—we're human" (83).

Tom Romano writes in *Blending Genre, Altering Style* that a multigenre paper "is composed of many genres and subgenres, each piece self-contained, making a point of its own, yet connected by theme or topic and sometimes by language, images, and content" (Romano 2000, x–xi). To prepare students to write their own multigenre papers, we practice genres they might include in their papers (see Figure 2–1).

Figure 2–1
Multigenre Assignment

Assignment: Write a multigenre paper in which you explain your life in Lockland or Arlington and how living in this community has shaped you and your dreams.

Length: 10–15 pages.

Due Dates: 3–4 pages—Thursday, 10/7
7–8 pages—Thursday, 10/14
Final draft—Wednesday, 10/20

Readings: *Life in the Ghetto,* "Life in Gangland," "Life in Siberia" (from *The Endless Steppe*), *Our America,* "Chicago," *The House on Mango Street, Parrot in the Oven*

Genres: These are suggestions, but everyone must include in their paper the ones that are <u>underlined</u>.

- <u>Character sketch</u> of neighbor/friend/family member
- Transcript of <u>interview</u> with relative/neighbor
- <u>Sketches</u> or <u>photos</u> of people/neighborhood
- <u>Dialog</u> with friend about an incident that strongly influenced your opinion of your neighborhood/school
- <u>Anecdote</u> that helps outsiders understand your neighborhood/school
- Dictionary of "Locklandisms"
- Tour of school/neighborhood
- Monolog about some aspect of growing up in a small town
- House-for-sale ad
- Essay from point of view of student from another school
- Advice column to younger sibling or new student about growing up in Lockland or fitting in at school
- Poem about your dreams and expectations
- Map of neighborhood
- Song lyrics (which you compose) that capture the mood or spirit of Lockland
- Other genres that help you explain/describe Lockland
- A variation of one of the suggested genres

Be creative! Don't be limited by these suggestions.

For example, they try a house-for-sale ad and a glossary of Locklandisms like the "Ghetto Glossary" Jones and Newman include in *Our America*. They read Carl Sandburg's "Chicago" and try a similar poem about Lockland. They brainstorm other genres that might help them portray life in Lockland, and then they answer these questions to prepare for their first conference with me:

1. Explain what you think will be the theme of your paper.

2. List some of the genres you plan on using and how you plan to use them (e.g., a dialog between you and your grandmother talking about how the school has changed since she graduated from here).

3. How do you plan to tie the paper together? Will certain voices or genres recur? Will you repeat a certain line?

4. Which 3–4 pages will you have drafted for the first conference this Thursday?

5. Since you filled this out earlier in the week and have now drafted 3–4 pages, what new ideas have occurred to you about your theme, the genres you'll use, or the shape your paper will take?

I set deadlines for students along the way because I know many of them will procrastinate if I don't. I know teachers who assign long-term projects that they expect students to work on independently and then are disappointed with the results. Working with students through the process helps them produce better drafts and meet assigned deadlines.

Halfway through this project I review with students some of the problems I notice in their emerging drafts—gaps that need to be filled, direct address that needs to be punctuated, or long prose passages that could be broken up into shorter ones (see Figure 2–2). As is the case with most minilessons, students take what they need and understand, ignoring advice that doesn't pertain or make sense to them. Again, I find that working with students through their writing process ensures better results in their final papers.

Andrew's and Desiree's final papers prove an interesting contrast. Desiree titles her paper "Home Is Where the Heart Is"; Andrew titles his "What's Wrong With Lockland?" Besides the title, his cover page includes a drawing of a "Welcome to Lockland" sign split down the middle. Both wrote house-for-sale ads. Desiree's reads:

> Three bedrooms, two full baths . . . a park located at the end of the street, school no more than a ten-minute walk . . . friendly neighbors . . . a safe environment . . . guaranteed to please. . . .

Andrew's is:

> Small, one story, one bedroom, one bath . . . located on the outskirts of Lockland . . . all new carpet and windows because of severe damage . . . will lower the price . . . need to leave as soon as possible.

Figure 2–2
Multigenre Papers in the Middle

Now that you're halfway done with your papers (at least in terms of time), consider some of the following as you continue drafting and revising:

- Putting pieces in order so they make sense to the reader (Some of your first pieces won't work in that position because they don't provide enough context for the reader to understand what is happening.)

- Tying pieces together so the paper is coherent (I noticed gaps in some of your drafts that will need to be filled in so other pieces make sense.)

- Separating pieces that address similar subject matter to surprise the reader (For example, one student has "Seven" and "Seventeen," about two birthdays, one right after the other—they might work better if they were apart.)

- Placing commas around names when you directly address someone (For example, "Yes, Joe, I heard you"—many of you used direct address in your paper.)

- Dividing up long prose passages (2–3 pages) into shorter ones that have more impact (If you dramatize a narrative summary, the reader will better experience what you did.)

- Writing more substantial pieces (Some of your drafts included 3–5 pages but none of the pages were more than a couple sentences—you need to include longer pieces that immerse readers in your topic so they identify with characters and subjects.)

- Typing drafts (You didn't need to have typed drafts this week, but time has been provided and your final does need to be typed.)

- Writing specifically (Some of you wrote diary or journal entries that were general—try to make all your writing specific.)

- Connect personally to your subject (Try not to distance yourself—the writing will be more interesting to both you and the reader.)

- Proofread, proofread, proofread (If you spend a month writing a paper that's personally meaningful, you don't want the final product to be full of mistakes.)

In Desiree's poem, modeled after Sandburg's "Chicago," she concedes that Lockland is overshadowed by Cincinnati, that the streets are torn and the buildings are tattered; no other place, however, is so worthy to be called her home. She maintains her positive outlook despite the negative attributes that Andrew spends his time focusing on. His poem compares the size of Lockland to a pea. He mentions the polluted Millcreek and the exodus of businesses, which has resulted in tax levies that "plague the school." Teenage pregnancy, [he says] "runs rampant." His advice: "Get out as soon as you can."

Both Andrew and Desiree include character sketches in their multi-genre papers. Desiree writes about Mrs. Weaver, a friend of her grandmother, who always had goodies for her and her sister, sometimes butterscotch candy, once stuffed teddy bears. Andrew writes about a homeless man he saw camped at the Millcreek—the polluted one he mentioned earlier—for whom he admitted feeling sorry. Andrew ends his character sketch by saying he fears that "many people in Lockland will end up like the man under the bridge."

The striking thing about these two writers is how they seem drawn to the positive or negative aspects of their hometown. Their attitudes shape their vision. Andrew probably had a Mrs. Weaver in his life, but he either could not or chose not to recall her. Desiree has no doubt seen a homeless person—perhaps the same one Andrew wrote about—but it wasn't him she chose to highlight. Both Andrew and Desiree include dialogs with friends in their papers. Desiree's revolves around the possibility of our school district merging with a neighboring district. Students staged a sit-in, invited the media, and protested the proposed merger. Desiree ends the dialog by saying she can still hear the chanting every time she walks into the gym. Andrew writes about a friend getting harassed by the "cops" after he was mistaken for someone else. "That's a bunch of bull crap," Andrew wrote. "I can't wait until I move."

At the end of the first semester, I asked students to compose a portfolio of their best writing to that point in the year. Besides revising and editing their revisions, they also had to write a reflective letter explaining the pieces they included. Desiree didn't include her multigenre paper, but she did reflect on the reading she did in preparation for the "Life in Lockland" paper:

> "Life in Gangland" by Sandra Gardner really opened my eyes. . . .
> I never realized life outside of Lockland could be so cruel. Those
> people are put through tough times every day. They have to be strong
> to survive. . . .

Reading about the "tough times" others endure helped Desiree appreciate her home and her life. Home *is* where her heart is. Andrew included his multigenre paper in his portfolio but then wrote this in his reflection:

> Multigenre papers are the most tedious and boring papers you will ever
> write. My multigenre paper was about the downside of Lockland. . . .
> The whole point of the paper was to criticize this town. I have never
> liked this town since I moved here and my writing reflects it.
>   In this paper I learned there are more faults in this town than I
> knew. . . . I also learned that Lockland ruined my childhood. There
> was nothing to do when I came here. It is the same way now. Hang-
> ing out on the street corners and at the same parks every day sucks.

It is ironic that Andrew claims multigenre papers are tedious and boring, yet when given the opportunity to reflect on his writing, includes it among the best in his portfolio. Using multiple genres helped him realize that there are "more faults" in this town than he knew. His paper expresses his vision of his town and his life. He is one of the most negative students I teach. Desiree, on the other hand, is one of the most positive. Her vision expresses that.

Multiple genres act as multiple lenses. Had she been writing a standard essay about her hometown, Desiree wouldn't have thought to write a recipe for a Lockland student that includes a pinch of diversity and a dose of small-town pride. Andrew wouldn't have written a letter to the mayor about the town's drug problems and corrupt police officers. Multiple genres help students see. Seeing helps them answer the question Who are you?

Family Relationships

After students have reflected upon the effect of place on identity, I ask them to write about family. I'm not trying to pry into their personal lives, but personal writing is important, especially for adolescents. They write best about that which they know; they enjoy writing about significant moments in their lives; they need to examine how those significant moments have shaped them. The risk is that other family members may not want some of those moments revealed. In my eighteen years of teaching, I've read dozens of revealing personal pieces, pieces about alcoholism and drug use, physical and verbal abuse. In some cases I've had to refer students to the counselor, or I've talked to the counselor myself. Never in all this time has a parent complained about these assignments. My guess is that most students don't share these pieces with their families. I do know of students, though, who have shared pieces about absent fathers with their single mothers. Still, no one has complained. If they did, I would defend such personal writing by saying that students have plenty of room to find topics within the parameters of the assignment. They know in advance that they'll be sharing their writing with their peers and me. They have the right to express themselves on paper.

At the same time, I don't want this assignment to threaten students, so I use Cynthia Heimel's "Diary of a Single Mother" as a model to get them started(Heimel 1996). Her diary recounts her struggle to raise her son alone. Each entry begins with a year, the first being 1970. In preparation for this piece, students draw a timeline and brainstorm significant familial events for as many years as they can remember. I suggest they record entries that they won't mind sharing with their peers and me. Then they look for patterns that will help them focus their writing. Tara chose abandonment, entitling her piece, "Diary of an Abandoned Daughter." Her story begins in 1979: "On November 16th I was born. My mother is there but my father isn't. I should bring happiness, but I don't." Tara relates only the events that shaped her life and support her theme.

In 1984 she recalls that her grandfather brings her doughnuts every morning before school. In 1985 he dies. Her father abandons her and her brother in 1987, but her mother gets a new boyfriend.

> 1988: We move in with my mother's boyfriend. He's an alcoholic, drug abuser. He beats my mother. My parents' divorce is final. My father becomes an alcoholic. But I never see him.

The boyfriend becomes so abusive that Tara and her family move in with her grandmother. Her father still isn't a part of her life and won't even accept pictures of her and her brother. Her mother remarries, but she and her new husband "fight a lot. There's never any peace." Another divorce, a new boyfriend, more moving, depression triggering thoughts of suicide, her father calling her brother more often now, "but [he] doesn't seem to remember me." Finally, to the present:

> I'm sixteen now. I have a job, a car, and my license, which I established for myself. I have a new best friend . . . I even call her mom "Mom." It's been over two years since I've told my real mom I love her. It's weird how you can love someone but not like them. I'm pretty much independent now. I have to be. I have a new boyfriend. He isn't at all like the other guys I've known. I quit relying on others to bring me happiness. I can do that for myself. I hope to go to college when I graduate. But my guess is my father won't be around to help.

Tara's "diary" ends there. She just graduated with a solid B average, the same boyfriend, and a baby of her own on the way. I wonder if this baby's father will be there for him (or her) or be the subject of another diary sixteen years from now. I've known countless young mothers since I've taught at Lockland. Many, like Tara, dream of their futures, aspire to a college education, claim their independence, and quit relying on others for their happiness. Most of them have to, unfortunately, because few of these young women marry their babies' fathers. Occasionally, they find ways to support their children as well as gain a college education. I hope Tara is one of them.

Using this format with short diary entries helps students focus on significant events that relate to one theme. Similar to the multigenre paper, each entry is like a slide in a slide show, working alone to provide readers with information, working together to immerse them in a theme. In Tara's case the abandonment is palpable.

I wish I could guarantee that writing about these experiences would break the cycles of abandonment and abuse. But I can't. I don't know what will become of Tara; I can only hope that when her baby is born, she will bring Tara the happiness that Tara didn't bring her own mother, that this baby will not have to lose its innocence so early in life.

Mimicking Voices

Sometimes writers need to try on other identities to find their own. When students read *The Catcher in the Rye*, they express their feelings about Holden, interpret his dream, analyze his attachment to mummies, and react to his desire to preserve Phoebe's innocence. But they also try on his voice. Instead of addressing the content of the book, though, I ask them to imagine Holden living today and to reflect on contemporary topics. Here's part of Mike's reflection:

> People are so phony anymore. . . . Always doing things just to look good. . . . Take . . . those goddamn morons that run our country. If they're not phony, who is?
>
> We've got this bastard Clinton in office. If he's not a bastard lacking morals, then I don't know who is. Think about it—gays in the military, gay rights. Who's he kidding? I'm practically an atheist and even I've read the Bible.
>
> The Bible . . . there's a damn good book. A little long but good. I may never have cared for the disciples and all, but that old Jesus sure was a character.
>
> Jesus, now there's a man with some morals. Had one of the roughest lives I've ever heard of, but not once did he sin. Old Jesus . . . I felt sorry and all for him, though, because no one ever believed him. He always seemed to have some type of problem. I've talked to Jesus, once or twice you know, just in case he is listening and all. I don't think you could call me faithful, at least not Noah faithful.
>
> Noah, now that was one faithful sonavubitch. I mean to build this big goddamn ark and all when it has never even rained before. . . .

When I asked Mike to write analytical pieces prior to this, he did just fine. Personal narrative was more difficult. This assignment freed him to express some of his own feelings, but through another's voice. I'm reminded of Kurt Vonnegut's short story "Who Am I This Time?" The protagonist Harry is shy, reserved, and quiet in public, nervous around other people, especially the opposite sex. When he takes the stage, though, he's dynamic, forceful, present. Asking our students to wear masks when they write can help them establish their voices. The opinions expressed in Mike's writing about politics and morals are not Holden's, but Mike's. In the end of Vonnegut's story, Harry finds romance; if Mike keeps writing, he'll find his voice.

Making Our Mark

Creating opportunities for students to write about their neighborhoods and families and to try on different voices helps them forge their own identities. Self-expression is what makes us human. We all need to leave our mark.

When I worked on the railroad, a friend pointed out a graffiti drawing on a passing boxcar. A man was slumped forward so his face didn't show. A huge sombrero covered his head. A striped blanket draped his body. Behind him grew a crooked palm tree. Underneath the drawing, written in script, was the artist's name—Herbie. I wasn't sure why my friend pointed this out to me. "Did he admire the artwork?" I wondered. But the next day I saw another boxcar with the same drawing. In fact, Herbie had left his mark on countless boxcars. Was he a brakeman working for the Chessie System? A vagrant riding the rails? We didn't know. But Herbie had left his mark as we all must. "Justin rules" on an expressway overpass; "Kilroy was here" in WWII; "Kelly Gibson— 1973," inked on a student desk. We each need to express our "self."

Eventually, though, our selves must interact with other selves. Through those interactions, we shape a new self for a new community. The classroom is one place where selves can be shaped. For the rest of this chapter, I'd like to share some of the evolving identities I've witnessed as students interact in the classroom. These interactions revolve around ethics and immigration.

Ethics and Identity

In Tom Perrotta's short story "Forgiveness," the narrator faces the biggest ethical dilemma of his life when his football coach asks the team whether Randy Dudley, one of the team's best players, should be forgiven so he can play in the state championship football game (Perrotta 1994). Randy had given his girlfriend a black eye, gotten drunk later that night, and wrecked his car after his girlfriend's father wouldn't let him talk to her. Though the policy was clear—drinking, smoking, and drug use were prohibited during the season, "get caught and you were gone"—the coach made a locker room speech about Christ and forgiveness just before the game was to be played. Though the narrator agrees with his best friend Rocky that Randy should not be forgiven, he wants the jacket that accompanies a state championship. So, along with the rest of his teammates, minus Rocky (who declines to play in the final game), he votes to "forgive" Randy, and his team wins the game by a touchdown.

My student teacher at the time, Tom Gaffigan, asked us to respond in round-robin fashion to the following question:

> Imagine yourself in the locker room at the end of the story when Coach Whalen asked the team to vote on whether Randy Dudley should be forgiven for violating team rules. If you were the narrator, how would you vote, especially in light of your best friend's decision to vote against forgiving Randy? Be sure to explain why.

When they'd completed their responses, Tom directed them to exchange papers with someone else who finished about the same time they did. After they responded to that writer, they exchanged with others for the entire fifteen-minute period. This dialog in writing gave them a chance to focus on the central dilemma of the story and see what each of their peers felt about the same topic. Keith said he liked the technique because it was a "good way for students to share their opinion without having others disrupt them while they were talking." I like it because everyone is involved. Even those who often remain silent in large-class discussions are engaged in round-robin responding. Even students with little to say can say it and know someone will respond to them. (I find they usually have more to say once the dialog begins.)

This is my initial response and the three responses I received from Rachle, Cliff, and Tom:

> If I had been in the narrator's shoes and only a sophomore in high school, I probably would've gone along with the team. However, I don't think I'd have been right. Rocky had guts. He knew "bullshit" when he smelled it and Coach Whalen's speech was bullshit. He liked using the flag and Vietnam and religion to get what he wanted, but I don't think he was really patriotic or religious. Sure, I believe in forgiveness, in being "Christ-like," but Randy Dudley beat his girlfriend; he needs to suffer the consequences. I would've voted to "forgive" Randy, but I would have been wrong.
>
> —J.G.

> I absolutely agree. The pressure of the team and wanting to win would have made me vote to forgive, even though it's not right.
>
> —Rachle

> I disagree. I wouldn't let a team or anyone influence me in what I thought. I believe in what's the better moral thing to do. The kid was arrested. I don't know about you, but I wouldn't want to play with a

criminal. Let's think about this. Football players are supposed to be "team leaders." Good players or not, "You play, you pay."

—Cliff

It's easy in retrospect to say I would have sided with Rocky. But, that would be as much BS as Whalen was shoveling. I agree with Mr. G. because the pressure of the moment would have made me cave in. I blame the adults in charge for not having the guts to exhibit the leadership for which they are paid. This should not have been in the players' hands.

—Tom Gaffigan

When we finished writing, Tom asked us to pass back the papers to the person who'd begun the response and to read our peers' comments. "Did anyone see a response that disagreed with what you'd written?" he asked. Nearly everyone's hand went up. Kristy said, "I think the narrator should've stuck by Rocky, but someone in here told me to 'lighten up,' that no one should hold 'grudges.' Well, I think they're wrong, that Randy deserved to be punished."

Julie said the dilemma in the locker room was never about "forgiveness" and shouldn't have been called a "vote": "This was just a way to get a star player back on the team for the championship game."

Charity identified with the "scrubs" in the story who'd been kicked off the team for drinking earlier in the season but never extended the same chance at forgiveness as Randy; they weren't good enough. Charity works her "butt off" for sports, attends every practice, only to see more talented athletes skip practice and still "earn" starting positions. She recognizes how policies are bent for a privileged few.

Justin said, "They won without Rocky, they could've won without Randy."

Rebecca claimed Coach Whalen needed a "reality check": "High school students are going to drink."

Through our oral and written responses, each of us establishes our identity. As an insecure high school student, I probably wouldn't have said a word had such a discussion taken place in my own high school English class (it never did because we never read stories like "Forgiveness"). Had I been pushed to respond, I would've said the "right thing" because I was a teacher-pleaser (probably the oldest-child syndrome). As a teacher far removed from adolescence, I could admit in my response now what I wouldn't have admitted then.

Rachle is a teacher-pleaser, too (also an oldest child). Cliff is the same student who said in Chapter 1 that rape is justifiable in war, yet in response to me here says he would do the "better moral thing," that he wouldn't be influenced by his teammates. But he understands Sergeant Meserve's men in Casualties of War consenting to rape to be part of the platoon/team.

Charity finds a personal connection. No one wants to admit being a "scrub," but Charity is more secure than most of her peers. She assesses her athletic talent realistically. She may be number two in her class academically, but athletically, she's a scrub.

Much of the identity formation in class discussion is posturing. Try out a line, see if it sticks. Get a laugh, strike a nerve. Garner support, challenge weakness. Be a "survivor." Take the high road (at least in public), jockey for position. Figure out who everyone else is, create an acceptable self.

Most of these students had been creating these "selves" together for ten or more years. They'd grown up in Lockland, shared classes since kindergarten. Not Daneesha.

Immigration and Race

Daneesha entered our school halfway through her junior year. Her skin was dark, her hair black, her eyes wide. She was one of two African American students in my Contemporary Culture class. Just prior to Daneesha coming to Lockland, students had finished papers they'd written about immigration. Billy (whose excerpts from "Life in Lockland" you read earlier) titled his paper, "Immigration Sucks" :

> My view on immigration is pretty well known to the rest of my class. I don't like immigration and think that we should close our borders for good. I'm very strongly opinionated on this topic. I hate going to stores and listening to this old Korean slope try to understand what I am saying. . . . I understand that in many countries that they are facing political coups and other problems, but to be frank that doesn't really concern me.

Billy doesn't mince words. His first sentence is right. His views are well known. His writing is often peppered with racial slurs, as is this one. Although he doesn't live in a particularly diverse community, he has encountered *some* diversity, and he doesn't like what he sees. His solution to illegal immigration: "Put up an electric fence on the border and instead of having our warships sit on the docks, have them sit in the Gulf of Mexico waiting for illegal immigrants who come on boats from Mexico and Cuba."

Billy did do some research for his paper. He found out how much is spent on illegal aliens. He broke that spending down into money allocated for Medicaid and for welfare. He reported that a significant portion of the prison population is made up of illegal immigrants. He read, much to his dismay, that if immigration continues at its present pace, that more than half the U.S. population will be nonwhite by 2050. So he concludes his paper like this:

We need to keep America pure. Keep it for the most part white. That way we can keep the majority of the smart people in office and the stupid slopes, spics, and other minorities out of office. I just want a safe and fair place for my children, my grandchildren, and their grandchildren to grow up. Their rights as white citizens will be stripped, and blacks and Hispanics and other minorities will have their way with the United States.

Papers like Billy's are not only troubling, but problematic. I want students to speak (and write) with honesty and confidence, but, as Peter McLaren writes, "How do [teachers] affirm these voices while at the same time questioning and challenging the racist . . . assumptions which inform them?" (Hynds 1997, 263). (I'll deal with this in greater detail in Chapter 3, "Prejudice: A Case Study.")

After reading all my students' arguments, I typed up excerpts on a one-page handout so they could reconsider their own views in light of their peers'. (I ask students early in the year if they mind me publishing anonymous quotes from their papers—so far, no one has objected.) Besides the two quotes from Billy's paper, the handout included these comments:

> It's crazy . . . we celebrate our immigrant heritage with parades and festivals . . . but then we blame our problems on the immigrants of today.

> Mexicans hurt the American people . . . by bringing over their problems and spreading them like a disease.

> The rich can't live with Mexicans and they can't live without them.

> Oftentimes, we try to push our drug and crime problems off on those less represented such as immigrants. I believe the first step is asking, "What have I done to prevent the selling of drugs and . . . crime in my community?"

> Most residents of the United States are too wrapped up in their own agendas and activities to even care about their fellow men and women that are in other countries suffering. They strive to survive off of crusts of bread that they find thrown in the streets for trash while we complain that the local McDonald's prices are too high. Are we really that insensitive and cruel?

> When I moved from Golf Manor to Lockland, it was as if I were an immigrant myself. I had to change my language, the way I dressed, the way I talked . . . the only difference is that I didn't leave my country, my family, my background, or my beliefs, just my friends and neighborhood. . . . Immigrants aren't socially equipped to fit in here.

> If the white population decreases, the problems in the U.S. will increase dramatically.

You can see from these quotes that Billy wasn't alone in his thinking about immigrants and immigration. Some of his peers felt differently than he did, but some of their comments echoed his. I passed out this handout the following day.

Daneesha's first day in Lockland.

For the other students in this class, we were following a pattern that had been established early in the year. Students enjoy this part of the writing process. Sometimes I ask them to read their papers aloud, sometimes I read them aloud myself, and sometimes I type excerpts on a handout. Each alternative provokes further thought and discussion, but seeing their peers' words before them usually works best. This was a new practice for Daneesha. A new school with new peers and a new teacher. She had to feel like an "immigrant" herself.

Billy's line about a "pure" America incensed her. She had to be wondering what kind of world she'd entered. Who were these people— these mostly white people? The majority of my new students rarely speak until they test the waters of class discussion, and it can take a while before they're willing to plunge in themselves. Daneesha, however, wasn't about to remain on the bank created by our circle of desks. She dove right in. How could anyone insist that white was "pure" she asked. A number of students wondered the same thing and called the comment stupid. Daneesha pointed to the question one student had asked about Americans being "insensitive and cruel" to reinforce her feelings about Billy's quote.

Carrie, who does not strike me as racist by any means, tried to deflect Daneesha's criticism by saying she understood the writer's concern for his children's safety, but she knew a white America wouldn't guarantee that. Daneesha interpreted Carrie's "defense" as bigoted, and before I knew it, discussion blazed like a fire out of control. When I tried to quiet the class, Daneesha yelled, "You said you wanted to hear what we think and now you won't let me talk!" It took time, but eventually everyone quieted, and I asked students to express their opinions about a "pure" America in writing. This is the best way I know to defuse a volatile discussion.

The following day I talked in private to Carrie, Daneesha, and Billy. Carrie was still hurt by Daneesha's attack on her, but I asked her to imagine how Daneesha felt being new to the school and attacked because she was black. She nodded as if she were beginning to understand. Billy was surprised his writing had elicited such a strong response from his peers. I asked him how he thought readers would react to "stupid slopes and spics," and he, too, nodded. He didn't change his position, but he recognized how inflammatory language could incite such passionate responses.

I told Daneesha that she now knew she had racist peers. "Not all," I said, "but some. I think we need to talk about race in class, though, if we're ever going to eliminate racism." She agreed, but said she was surprised that so many of her peers were prejudiced. I told her as we walked toward the computer lab that while seven of her peers agreed with the "pure America" quote in the postdiscussion writing they'd done, thirteen disagreed. Marie, the other African American student in class, walked with us. She said she was surprised that only seven people agreed. "Especially since it was a secret ballot," she said. Daneesha was still upset—"Even one is too many."

This class was a risk but a risk I'd take again. Susan Hynds writes, "As teachers, I believe we silence too many conversations, in our fear of stepping out of the politically neutral perspective assigned to us by society" (Hynds 1977, 266). I don't know how else I can help students become aware of the power of language if they can't test their words on their peers in the classroom. Constructing effective arguments means paying attention to audience. As Goodman points out, "strong communities are not necessarily built from the 'homogeneous consensus' of all residents" (Hynds 1977, 266–267).

I reminded them of a board meeting earlier that year when our school discussed merging with an adjacent district. A resident from the neighboring town declared at the meeting that his community didn't want Lockland's "problems," a code word for blacks. He'd been booed out of the cafeteria. Then I told students to reread the quote about Mexican "problems . . . spreading like a disease," and reminded them that they'd rejected a similar argument when it concerned their own school. Some argued that the analogy didn't work, but it did make most of them pause.

Herbie's mark—his boxcar drawing—is one-dimensional; the world is not. His drawing of a slumped-over Mexican reflects a racist stereotype; ours must not. The self we construct must reflect our interactions with people different from ourselves. The marks Daneesha and Billy make cannot exist in isolation because our mark and theirs must be dynamic and multidimensional.

Like the world we live in.

3

Prejudice—A Case Study

TEACHING STRATEGIES

- *Brainstorming stereotypes*
- *Challenging assumptions*
- *Prompting rethinking*
- *Four Corners*
- *Teacher modeling*
- *Extending conversations*
- *Rethinking through portfolios*

"Sick, they really make me sick."

Misty

"If we hope to get students to rethink (rather than merely repress) what strike us as disturbing positions . . . we need first to find ways of keeping them an active part of the conversation of the class."

Joseph Harris (1995, 37)

Empathy and Prejudice

My daughter Kelly's favorite game at five years old was "Shoestore," which she played every time she visited Grandma or Daba. Kelly loved walking in her grandmothers' shoes. Students will walk in different shoes, too, and teachers can help. Not as "salespeople," pushing one

31

brand to the exclusion of others, but as "grandparents," rummaging around in our literary closets, searching for "shoes" our students might wear. Walking through literature helps students realize what Scout does at the end of *To Kill a Mockingbird:* that you can't understand others "until you stand in [their] shoes and walk around in them" (Lee 1960, 282). Before we can help students, though, we need to uncover the roads that they've walked.

Misty reveals the path she's been walking in her "Life in Arlington" paper:

> I can remember my mom swapping seeds with an elderly lady that lived down the street from us. Her name was Mrs. Cook. She lived in a really old run-down house with her daughter Jean. . . . Both my mom and Mrs. Cook always had nice yards. Maybe that's because of all the swapping seeds business. Really Mrs. Cook didn't have that much. The only things she had left when her husband passed away was her daughter, a scrungy little mutt named Gigi, and her precious flowers. I guess when you don't have much, you learn to cherish the little you do have.

From this early piece I learn that even when Misty was young, she tried on different people's shoes. She understood what Mrs. Cook had, and, by comparison, what she and her family had. She recognized economic disparity even if she couldn't name it. She empathized with Mrs. Cook and witnessed her own mother's kindness.

Misty signed up for my Contemporary Culture class the first semester of her senior year. She had transferred to Lockland as a sophomore after attending a Catholic girls' school nearby. She offered her peers and me a different perspective, gained through a private, homogeneous education. Being different at Lockland sometimes proves a liability, but most students accepted Misty immediately. Her smile is warm, her green eyes, inviting. Soft-spoken, sometimes quiet, Misty is friendly and popular. This year her senior classmates chose her as their homecoming queen.

One of the purposes of Contemporary Culture is to help students explore their assumptions about contemporary issues and the origin of those assumptions. Misty's paper helped me understand where she's walked and where she stands now. I hope viewing issues from different perspectives will help her and her peers rethink initial views, even if they eventually return to the comfort of their own shoes.

The better acquainted Misty and I became, the more I appreciated her ability to empathize. That, and the fact that her stance on most issues mirrored mine, reassured me that at least I was connecting with one student. From gender to patriotism, we'd seen eye to eye. What happens, though, when the values constructed by teachers' and students' assumptions conflict? Do I have the right to pry them out of their comfortable shoes? Can I offer alternatives without selling a prepackaged set of different beliefs?

The Contact Zone

I think I can. Not by being didactic, certainly, but by nudging them, hoping they'll consider alternative points of view. Mary Louise Pratt calls this space where a student and teacher's ideologies conflict the "contact zone," a place "where cultures meet, clash, and grapple with each other, often in highly asymmetrical relations of power" (Pratt 1991, 34). More and more often I find myself working in this zone, struggling to find ways to address difference without stifling voices.

Lately, I've felt schizophrenic. On the one hand I'm pleased; students are expressing themselves honestly. On the other, I'm torn: how can I help students improve writing while simultaneously considering prejudices and insensitivities? Take, for instance, a racist piece. I don't want to suggest students add more specific examples of how they've been racist to "improve" their writing.

This is the dilemma I explore in the following case study. From the Misty I got to know through her "Life in Arlington" to her revisions of a different piece, I trace the effects of reading, writing, and talking on Misty's thinking.

A unit on race and class proved the fork where our value paths diverged. Students and I begin this unit by brainstorming myths about race and class: "People on welfare are lazy" and "Native Americans are alcoholics" were two from a long list the semester Misty took my class. If we hope to have an honest discussion of our differences, we have to explore students' initial assumptions. I hope that during the course of our reading, writing, viewing and talking, students will begin to challenge some of these myths. For example, one essay we read, called "What Is Poverty?" (Parker 1989), shows students that some welfare mothers seek gainful employment, but lack of day care and transportation narrow their window of opportunity. Misty admits she "never had a clear picture" of poverty until reading the essay. Thinking about "pee-stained mattresses," the "unbearable smell of sour milk," and "suffering" children makes her wonder if she could survive what the woman endures: "It's strange how placing yourself in someone else's shoes can change the way you feel about a whole issue," Misty writes, "but I'm proof that it can."

Our study culminates with a paper about some aspect of race and/or class. Since we had read and discussed so many multicultural voices, I assumed students would empathize with those different from them. With Misty (and a number of other students) I was wrong.

Narratives and Prejudice

Misty wrote a piece about a summer vacation to Florida, beginning innocently enough with a brief description of the drive down interstate 75, then offering a hint of the impending conflict: "Why are there so many damn Michigan drivers on the road? I guess you could say that was a prejudiced thought, but hey, aren't we all a bit prejudiced?" The ride becomes more integral to the story than I first suspected:

> I laugh at mom's head bobbing, sleeping, a loud pitter-pattering coming up slowly on the right side, what is that God awful noise?—look back only to see a piece of shit truck moving along the best it can with low tires, back end waited (sic) down by melons and tomatoes, smoke pouring out the tailpipe, and a stench making my stomach turn. . . .
>   . . . LATINOS, a truck full of LATINOS
> Sick, they really make me sick. . . .

The last line defied my expectations. The Misty I'd gotten to know (who admits it would be difficult leaving the nursing home she works in because she'd miss the patients) not only empathized with others but treated them kindly. How could this truck full of Latino men sicken her? The next excerpt provides an explanation:

> Winn Dixie last summer
>   me . . . and a bunch of LATINOS, trying to exit the store, getting catcalled—"Hey chica, you want some of this Big Papa?"
>   YUCK!
>   As I make my way through, a tongue shoots in and out of a mouth violently at me, almost like a snake—ready for attack.
>   Repulsed . . .
>   I leave highly bothered, unable to concentrate, wanting to punch anyone that crossed my path, shaken and afraid.

I hadn't known Misty had been sexually harassed. I imagined her scared and threatened, hurrying to escape this verbal barrage. Still, to stereotype an entire race based on one incident counteracted all the work she and my other students had done demythologizing their original assumptions.

Misty makes a sophisticated writing move in her next paragraph juxtaposing past and present:

> The truck gradually moves closer. Staring in . . . I see dirty men—arms covered with the earth that brought them their soul (sic) income, the dirt that fed their kids . . . but still they were dirty and gross.
>   "Get a real job!"
>   I saw many LATINOS on the trip down, many selling fruit on the sides of the road, all dirty.

> I didn't think of their lives, only of the day at the market, the pulsating tongues, and the rude catcalls.
>
> . . . "Isn't it a shame to hate a race because of a couple people?" I thought about it. . . . "Yeah, it is, but what the hell."
>
> My head rolls over and I dream of the beach.

After reading what Misty had written earlier about her mother and Mrs. Cook, "Get a real job!" stung. It didn't seem to me that Misty was "placing herself in someone else's shoes."

To say this paper proved problematic is an understatement. It is, in fact, a perfect example of Pratt's contact zone. In her work Pratt theorizes a teaching practice that asks students (and teachers) to examine cultural and linguistic differences instead of ignoring them.

How to implement such a practice concerned me. My role as a writing teacher demands that I help students improve their writing—show them how to express their views more clearly, support those views with detailed examples, unify and organize their thoughts, and employ the conventions of standard written English.

My role doesn't end there, though. I believe in democracy, in an educated citizenry. I believe our country (and my classroom) should be inclusive and that each of us should tolerate and appreciate difference. I'd like to see students embrace these values. But I have to be careful. I don't have the right to impose my views on anyone.

I do hope, though, I can convince students that examining their beliefs is worthwhile. At the same time I'd like to see them critique American institutions such as slavery or an unfair justice system and challenge or even resist dominant ideologies. Geoffrey Chase (1990, 31) writes in "Perhaps We Need To Just Say Yes," that "resistance is not only a way of saying 'no' to the dominant culture, but a way of saying 'yes' to an alternative vision of the culture which is more truly democratic."

I agree and hope to foster such a vision in my own classes. I want my students to venture beyond the community of the classroom, to risk their voices in the public sphere, to "push against the boundaries of an oppressive social order" (Giroux 1992, 141).

The problem for me with Misty's resistance is that her alternative vision is not more democratic, and the linguistic risks she takes in her paper maintain the status quo. Misty is not the marginalized Latino laborer whose voice is drowned out by conservative politicians. But just because her politics, at least on this issue, run to the right of mine, can I dismiss them the way she does Latinos?

The asymmetrical relations of power inherent in any teacher-student relationship further complicate my role (and that of any teacher working in the contact zone). Eventually, I have to grade Misty's paper. She knows that and so do I.

Prompting Rethinking

The dilemma for me, on the one hand, is encouraging Misty to keep writing, consider revision, and examine her assumptions, while on the other, convincing her to do so without compromising herself and the integrity of her paper. I won't tell Misty what to think, but I can encourage her to rethink.

In my written response to her paper, I praise her ability to describe what she experienced, ask her if the "real job" comment is fair, and at the end of the paper next to her dismissive response write, "Would you want someone to dismiss you the way you dismiss them?"

The following day I took my students to the computer lab. As students began revising and editing their papers, Misty and I talked.

"You know, Misty, a lot of people make racist or sexist comments and never realize it, but at the end of your piece, you show you're very aware of your prejudices. Despite that," I say pointing to the end of her paper, "you still blow it off and think about the beach. Can you tell me what you were thinking there?"

Misty brushes a strand of hair from her eyes and says, "Yeah, I was trying to show that a lot of people think it's easier not to think about being prejudiced. They realize it's wrong, but what can they do about it? I felt guilty thinking what I did, but everyone's prejudiced, don't you think?"

"Probably so," I reply nodding my head. "I guess I didn't see any guilt coming through in your paper. Let me ask you about something else. What if the boys outside the store had been white? Have you ever been harassed in the same way by white guys?"

"Yeah," Misty nods. "My mom says why not take it as a compliment, but I think it's degrading."

"Has your opinion about white men been shaped the same way it is about Latinos in your paper?"

Misty's eyes sparkle and a smile crosses her face. "No, I guess that's prejudiced right there, isn't it?"

"Why do you suppose your reaction is different?" I ask her.

"I guess because I relate to whites easier because I'm white."

"Maybe you can think about some of the things we've been talking about as you revise your paper, okay?" Misty nods her head, takes her draft to a computer, and begins revising.

The next day I collect students' revisions. Misty makes two major changes in this draft, which she now titles "Memories of a Summer." In between the boy's "catcall" and wedging her way through the crowd, she inserts a passage describing the boy's appearance and her feelings about him:

A teenage boy, sweat pouring off his brow, walking with a strut, shirt half-unbuttoned, gold chain with a marijuana leaf dangling from it, dew rag on his head, and an attitude that made you want to smack him across his face. His eyes peer right through me, and I feel he is undressing me with his glare . . . I want to get away.

The second change occurs at the end of the paper:

"Isn't it a shame to hate a race because of a couple people?" I thought about it . . . *Guilt-ridden*, I think, "Yeah, it is, but what the hell." [My emphasis]
My head rolls over and I dream of the beach.

Both changes address Misty's feelings about what happened to her outside the Winn-Dixie. The second acknowledges the guilt she told me she felt, and the first rationalizes it. Though the hyphenated adjective is a simplistic way of expressing her guilt, Misty's revisions communicate her feelings more clearly. She seems to be saying, "If you didn't understand before, dear reader, why I feel as I do, you should now. No one should have to endure this kind of harassment."

Though Misty doesn't address the way she stereotypes the men in the truck, she believes her revision better explains why she feels as she does. Even though I believe her prejudice is still unwarranted, intellectually I understand how her feelings evolved. Misty's story reminds me of one of my own.

Rethinking Ourselves

Most of what I learned about African Americans growing up in the predominantly white suburbs south of Pittsburgh was negative. The same sorts of myths my students brainstormed at the beginning of this unit were even more pervasive then. Not until I moved to New Brunswick, New Jersey, in fifth grade did I actually meet a black student.

My new-school nervousness doubled that first day in the cafeteria because I feared my black peers. Squeezing between two tables of students bent over their lunches, I felt a pin prick my right buttocks. I turned abruptly to see the smiling face of a black boy, right hand bearing the straight pin he'd used to stick me. Everything I'd learned about blacks in Pittsburgh was confirmed for me with that one sharp sting. It took years of lived experience, of reading about African Americans, of being inspired by Martin Luther King, to undo that tiny pinprick, which shaped my fifth-grade mind-set. Watching Gregory Peck's Atticus Finch in the black-and-white film version of *To Kill a Mockingbird* played a pivotal role in my own evolution. Awed by his brilliant defense of Tom

Robinson, the all-white jury's guilty verdict devastated my fourteen-year-old consciousness.

Considering the years it took for my own attitude toward African Americans to change helped me realize that I needed to continue the dialog Misty and I had begun, to keep her and all my students discussing and reconsidering their prejudices. Joseph Harris (1995, 37) writes that the contact zone is more like a process than a physical space, "a local and shifting series of interactions among perspectives and individuals." I've always liked the idea of process, and "shifting perspectives" sounds like the shoes I invite my students to walk around in. So how can I keep the conversation alive in my own classroom?

Extending the Conversation

After students revised their papers, I showed them the film *El Norte,* about two Guatemalan peasants who seek refuge in "the North" after government guerrillas murder their parents. Their journey through Mexico and across the border is fraught with danger, but Enrique and Rosa risk their lives for the freedom they imagine awaits them in California. Unfortunately, the world they envision proves anything but ideal. Entering the world of Enrique and Rosa helps students imagine the plight of illegal aliens.

This is important for Misty because, as we see from her journal response, it gives her "the capacity to invent visions of what should be and what might be deficient in our society" (Greene 1995, 5):

> After watching *El Norte,* I have changed my views a little. Before seeing this movie, I felt that immigration was a bad thing. I didn't think that people should be able to come to the U.S. and take our jobs. Then I tried to place myself in their shoes.

Although Misty was able to do that, some of her peers could not. After viewing the film, we played a game called Four Corners (see Figure 3–1). Students assumed one of the following positions about immigration and went to a designated corner:

1. Illegal immigration should be stopped.
2. Illegal aliens with jobs should be permitted to stay.
3. Quotas should be raised so more people can immigrate legally.
4. Quotas should be lowered; the U.S. has too many new immigrants.

Unlike a finite game, where the purpose is to win, Four Corners is an infinite game, where the purpose is to continue playing to explore other positions. This game helps students articulate their own

Figure 3–1
Four Corners

Unlike a finite game, which has as its purpose winning, Four Corners is an infinite game, which has as its purpose continuing play. These are some variations and rules for the game.

A topic, in the form of an assertion, is written on the board. For example, "Illegal immigrants should be sent back to their country of origin." Students decide if they *strongly agree, agree, disagree,* or *strongly disagree* with that statement. Then they might do one of the following before beginning the game:

- Write for five minutes before going to the corner of the room that best reflects their opinion.
- Meet in small groups with peers who feel the same way about the topic and discuss why they believe as they do.
- Write and then meet with peers in small groups.
- Go to one of the four corners of the room and immediately begin the game.

A variation of the game is to offer four different positions related to the same topic. For example, students might consider these opinions about illegal immigration:

1. Illegal immigration should be stopped.
2. Illegal aliens with jobs should be permitted to stay.
3. Quotas should be raised so more people can immigrate legally.
4. Quotas should be lowered; the U.S. has too many new immigrants.

Students could then write, meet in groups, or begin the game.

Some rules for the game:

- Go to the corner that best represents your opinion.
- Don't try to choose the "right" position.
- Know why you believe as you do.
- Communicate your opinion clearly to your peers.
- Listen closely to your peers' opinions.
- Only one person is permitted to talk at a time.
- Respect other peoples' opinions.
- Don't insult or attack peers who think differently than you.
- Move to another corner if your opinion changes.
- Be ready to explain why you moved.

(*continued on page 40*)

Figure 3–1 (continued)
Four Corners

To end the game, students should return to their desks and write again for five minutes, reflecting on what they heard and what they think now about the topic and the game. They might consider these questions:

- Did you hear an argument that made sense to you?
- Are you closer to understanding why you think what you think?
- Did you hear anything you didn't expect to hear?
- Were you surprised by how your peers positioned themselves?
- Did you think about moving to another corner?
- Is there another position on this topic that makes more sense to you? If so, state it and explain your reasoning.
- If you were going to write a paper or make a speech about this topic, what research might you do to help you make a convincing argument?
- Did you enjoy the game? Did it make you uncomfortable?
- Did you learn anything?
- Would you like to play Four Corners again?

---

arguments, refute the arguments of others, and understand the importance of audience.

As part of this particular audience, Misty was surprised by the arguments she heard:

> I couldn't believe how my own friends could turn away someone like Enrique and Rosa . . . after they fought so hard. . . . I didn't realize how cold-hearted even one of your best friends could be. That could be me that she would have sent back to a country with no home.

In "Fault Lines in the Contact Zone," Richard Miller writes, "Required self-reflexivity does not, of course, guarantee that repugnant positions will be abandoned. At best, it ensures only that the students' attention will be focused on the interconnections between the ways they read and the ways they write" (Miller 1994, 407).

Rethinking Through Portfolios

To help students focus on those interconnections, I ask them to submit a portfolio at the end of the course (see Figure 3–2). The portfolio gives them a chance to review their reading and writing and to reflect upon what they've learned. As Maxinie Greene (1995, 65) writes,

Figure 3–2
Contemporary Culture Final Portfolio

The theme of the class this semester was "Our America: Image and Voice." The purpose was to help you understand the images and voices that represent America from the present and past, your own and other American communities. The reading and writing you did was to help you develop your own voice and explore how your community and school, your family and peers, have shaped your voice. For this final assignment, compose a portfolio that represents that exploration and development.

Part I

Choose three pieces of writing from this semester that best reflect your writing ability. Revise the pieces, proofread, and edit the final drafts. For one of the pieces, include all the drafts and peer and teacher comments. Consider the following pieces:

- the "pigeon" poem
- the character sketch
- the multigenre paper
- the prejudice paper
- the "forgiveness" paper
- any other writing from the course that you think is your best

Part II

Choose five to ten additional items that best reflect your learning this semester. Include voices and images in your portfolio that reflect contemporary America. Think about some of the following:

- brainstorming myths
- "Pigeons"
- "Life in Gangland"
- Our America
- "Forgiveness"
- map of Lockland
- "What Is Poverty?"
- *El Norte*
- Four Corners

(*continued on page 42*)

Figure 3–2 (continued)
Contemporary Culture Final Portfolio

Letter

In a "Dear Class" letter, please explain each item in your portfolio. Why did you include these pieces and not others? How do they represent your learning this semester? Be specific and thorough.

In Part I explain how the one piece that includes all the drafts has changed since you began it—be specific. You should highlight sections that have changed from the first to final draft and refer specifically to those changes and what prompted them. Why is the piece better now? Explain, too, what you've learned about editing. What mistakes do you continue to make? How have you learned to correct them for this portfolio? Note at least three errors.

In Part II consider the course content. Remember the theme of the course—*Our America: Image and Voice*. Try to find items that represent the images and voices—local and distant, present and past—that you saw and heard this semester. Write a reflective letter that represents those images and voices. Reflect on your attitude toward Lockland as expressed in your Life in Lockland paper: Is the tone hopeful, critical, positive, negative, proud, embarrassed, hostile, regretful, apathetic, sincere, joking, or something else? Do you think growing up in a different community would make you a different person in any way? A different American? What did you learn about yourself and your peers from the unit on race and class? What do you know now that you didn't know before?

Guidelines

1. Each paper in Part I should be revised, edited, and typed—one paper should include all drafts stapled together with the first draft on the bottom and the final one on top.
2. A table of contents should be prepared.
3. Your portfolio should be neatly organized.

TURNING IN A PORTFOLIO IS REQUIRED TO PASS THE COURSE!

". . . teachers must . . . emphasize the importance of persons becoming reflective enough to think about their own thinking and become conscious of their own consciousness." Misty does that as she reflects on a number of artifacts, among them these:

1. "Memories of a Summer"
2. "My Life in Arlington"

3. journal response to *El Norte*
4. list of myths about race and class

She reflects in her "Dear Class" letter about the significance of each item:

> Last summer while shopping in a grocery store I was approached by a Latino boy who said really rude things to me . . . [which] made me feel ashamed and violated. From that point on I have felt uncomfortable around Latino people. I'm not real sure how one person's actions can change the way you feel towards an entire race, but it happened to me. Now I can understand how blacks feel hatred towards whites. . . .
>
> In a way this incident . . . makes me feel a little nervous around all men. No one should have to feel the way I did that day at the market. It gives you a feeling of insecurity. It made me feel almost paranoid to leave the house without double-checking my clothes to see if what I was wearing might get me "in trouble." I feel that incident took something away from me—that being my ability to see Latinos as an equal to me.

Misty's conclusion interests me. She recognizes her prejudice but expresses confusion about how such prejudices evolve. At the same time she admits clearer understanding of blacks' feelings towards whites. She offers additional information about her insecurities and surprises me by characterizing as a *loss* her ability to see Latinos as equal. Misty wishes things were different but at least for now can't shake the way one incident makes her feel.

Reflecting further in her portfolio letter, Misty writes that our conference helped her revise her paper. "Simply by asking me questions that I hadn't really thought about, Mr. Gaughan helped me to think about what I wrote and why I wrote it." Jack Thompson says, "If we know what we know, and if we know how we came to know it, we are powerful people" (Thompson 1993, 133). Misty was rethinking, rewriting, and reconsidering first thoughts. In the process, becoming a more powerful person.

About *El Norte* Misty writes that the "movie helped me realize how fortunate I am to live in the country that I do," just as she realized the relative comfort she and her family enjoyed in relation to Mrs. Cook. Regarding the list of myths, Misty adds, "I realized that these really were myths and stupid assumptions that people make based on a lack of knowledge." Finally, the last paragraph of her letter:

> The goal of this class was to try to look at things from all different aspects. I can honestly say that I feel that I am able to do that now. It's hard to change your opinions that have been instilled in you from the beginning, but if you try, you can see how other people feel, too. You

never know how another person is feeling unless you have tried to put yourself in their shoes.

Richard Miller writes, "For teachers who believe in education as a force for positive social change . . . the most promising pedagogical response [to students writing in the contact zone] lies . . . in closely attending to what our students say and write in an ongoing effort to learn how to read, understand, and respond to the . . . multivocal texts they produce" (Miller 1994, 408).

Walking with Misty through the contact zone has reminded me of my own prejudices—how they were constructed in Pittsburgh, reinforced in New Jersey, addressed in my reading, and readdressed now. Like Joseph Harris, I want to urge student writers not to "simply defend the cultures into which they were born but to imagine new public spheres which they would like to have a hand in making" (Harris 1995, 39).

For that to happen all of us must reexamine our assumptions and biases and how they evolved. I think Misty is on her way. She's acknowledged her prejudices, an important first step. She's explored the connections between two separate events. She's described how she was made to feel and how those feelings transferred to people she's never met. For now, the pinprick of prejudice still stings Misty. Perhaps with more experience the pain will fade.

4

Cultural Representation

TEACHING STRATEGIES
- *Brainstorming cultural images*
- *Juxtaposing cultural texts*
- *Immersion in cultural themes*
- *Imagination and cultural reflection*

When Euro-American writers "take on" one of my cultures, I feel quite violated. It is a form of cultural imperialism—the euphemism for cultural rape.

Thela Seto (1995, 171)

[If] certain stories may only be told by certain people . . . it would result in authors only being able to write their own story over and over.

Kathryn Lasky (1996, 4)

To arbitrarily set borders for our writers, boxing them in with rules, is to do literature the gravest disservice.

Jane Yolen (1994, 705)

Representing Other Cultures

Jane Yolen admits to being "an empress of thieves." She "borrows" characters, settings, and plots from other cultures, all the while realizing that "borrowing is a hazardous occupation." She understands the "necessity for research—cultural, physical, historical" (Yolen 1994, 703). Thelma Seto, a Japanese-American writer, read Ms. Yolen's "An Empress of Thieves" with "great consternation." According to Seto, "it is morally wrong for Euro-American writers to 'steal' from other cultures in order to jump on the multicultural bandwagon, unless they have direct, personal experience in the country where that culture originates— more than simply being a tourist or doing research in the library" (Seto 1995, 169). Kathryn Lasky writes:

> By the new rules of this multicultural game, I would be destined to keep writing about Midwestern Jewish girls of Russian extraction. . . . What if I wanted to write a novel about a Sephardic Jew? Am I to be told that I can never capture the Sephardic voice? That this is a voice parched by the winds of North Africa, salted by the brine of the Mediterranean, forged in the pressure cooker of the Spanish Inquisition. My family is not Sephardim, nor are they Eshkenazy Jews. At this rate, I would never get west of Warsaw. (Lasky 1996, 5)

Lasky's own experience as a reader tells her to resist these new rules: *The Diary of Anne Frank* "profoundly moved" her; Elie Wiesel's "harrowing novel" *Night* "seared her"; but it was William Styron's *Sophie's Choice* that touched her soul and "stirred me more deeply" (Lasky 1996, 6). If William Styron, a non-Jewish writer, could make such an impact on a Jewish reader, then Lasky should be entitled to write about people who aren't Midwestern Jews of Russian extraction.

This debate is not something that just plays itself out on the pages of *The Horn Book* or *The New Advocate*, of interest only to scholars and critics and writers. Consider popular culture and the movie *Amistad*. Haki Madubuti, owner of Third World Press, is quoted in *Newsweek* as saying, "We have to be in control of our own stories—just like our destinies. I'm not saying that [Steven] Spielberg isn't capable of making a decent film about blacks. What I'm saying is that blacks should be given first chance at our own stories" (Ansen and Samuels 1997). What's interesting about the *Newsweek* story is the parenthetical advice immediately following Madubuti's quote: "For a stunning film about slavery by a black director, rent Charles Burnett's 1996 'Nightjohn'" (65). Ironically, the popular young adult author Gary Paulsen—who happens to be white—wrote the novel upon which that movie is based.

Two other classic white authors have depicted African American experience to critical acclaim: Harper Lee and Mark Twain. Some critics, however, now regard Twain's depiction of Jim in *Huck Finn* as such a misrepresentation that many teachers opt not to teach it. Ralph Ellison (1964, 72) found Jim to be "a white man's inadequate portrait of a slave." Fredrick Woodard, from the University of Iowa, traces Twain's portrayal of Jim to the "swaggering buffoonery of the minstrel clown"

(Woodard and MacCann 1992, 145). This is the same book T. S. Eliot named a "masterpiece" and the novel from which, Ernest Hemingway says, "all modern American literature comes."

The controversy surrounding *Huck Finn* is familiar to most English teachers. *To Kill a Mockingbird,* though, does not share as controversial a history. Yes, it has been challenged because of the word *nigger*—as has Twain's classic—but Tom Robinson isn't a "buffoon." Still, is Harper Lee's portrayal of the Depression-era South an accurate representation or a white liberal one? Tom isn't a slave as Jim is, but he isn't an active agent in obtaining his own civil rights either. Jim is freed because of Miss Watson's benevolence; Tom, a "silent victim," needs a white lawyer's voice to gain his freedom.

In his provocative essay "Racism and Huckleberry Finn: Censorship, Dialogue, and Change," Allen Carey-Webb (1993, 33) argues that "no teacher should be required to teach this novel [*Huck Finn*]" because *nigger* is used and that "educating white students about prejudice with a text that is alienating to blacks perpetuates racist priorities." If works such as *Huck Finn* are used in the curriculum, Carey-Webb says that teachers must teach students to think "critically about literature, history, politics, and language" (28).

When I've taught *Huck* or other texts that include racially offensive epithets, my students and I discuss the importance of language in context. Gloria Naylor's "Mommy, What Does 'Nigger' Mean?" helps introduce this concept. Naylor is an African American writer who explains in her essay that the first time she "heard" the word was in elementary school when one of her peers used it to disparage her. Upon additional reflection, she realized she'd heard the word regularly from family members, but always in different contexts, never to offend as this little white boy had intended. Naylor's essay helps us understand the importance of intent and of the relationship between the speaker/writer and listener/reader. That same word doesn't always convey the same meaning. In fact, Naylor discusses a number of meanings for the word, even as it is used among different members of her family.

We also read Countee Cullen's poem "Incident," in which the narrator discusses a trip to Baltimore, where, despite all the other sights and sounds, he remembers only one word—"nigger." His story is like Gloria's. It reinforces the power of a six-letter word upon young, impressionable ears. By coupling the poem and story, students recognize the power of the word to offend and, at the same time, appreciate the importance of context.

The problem with the "n" word (and other culturally sensitive language) is that not all African Americans (or members of a culture) feel the same way about its use. Some rap artists use the word in their song lyrics. Some audience members find it offensive. Some say "nigga" is different than "nigger." No one member of a culture speaks for an entire culture. There is no such thing as an "accurate representation" of all the members of any culture. The best teachers can do when they teach literature such as *Huck* is to discuss language in context beforehand and insist that we all be respectful.

Brainstorming Cultural Images

Helping students to think critically is one of my most important teaching goals, so I've decided not to exclude controversial texts (in this case texts written by authors not of a particular culture), but to pair them with texts written by people from that culture. I wondered if cultural representation would matter to my students as it has to the critics I've quoted. What if the author using "nigger" were African American? What if a "drunken Indian" appears in a short story written by a Native American? What if a woman writes about a man?

My student teacher Amy Wilson and I began our study by asking students in our Contemporary Culture class to brainstorm their impressions of Native Americans. Micah said he thought of "warriors," "Sitting Bull," and "sidekicks" (Tonto, I suppose). "I think Indians are religious," he said.

Nikki added "ritualistic. I think they're intelligent and truthful, too, but they aren't portrayed that way."

"How are they portrayed?" I asked.

"Like banshees running around fires with their hands over their mouths."

"Are there other portrayals in popular culture that mirror what Nikki said?" I asked the class.

"Chief Wahoo, the Cleveland Indians' mascot, is cartoonish," responded Matt.

"Those images are wrong!" Nathan insisted. "Some of my ancestors were Native American, and that's not how we are. I wish I would've lived back when we were free. Native Americans had pride and heart."

Juxtaposing Cultural Texts

I asked the students to read two stories, "Lark Song," by W. P. Kinsella, and "Amusements," by Sherman Alexie. Kinsella is white Canadian and Alexie is Spokane Indian, but I didn't tell students that until after they read the stories. My intention wasn't to deceive them, but I didn't want to color their readings either. Silas Ermineskin, a Cree Indian who narrates a number of Kinsella's stories, narrates "Lark Song." This particular story focuses on his brother Joseph, "22 already, but when he just a baby he catch the scarlet fever and his mind it never grow up like his body do. . . . He be gentle and never hurt nobody in his whole life" (Kinsella 1986, 114). When Joseph hears a song, he can play it on his guitar, but he quickly forgets it. Silas admires Joseph's ability to sound like birds, especially the meadowlark, which makes "the prettiest sound of any bird I ever heard" (115). Their father is a drunk who sometimes disappears for a week at a time, and Silas admits he and his friends occasionally go to town to get "a beer or two." One time they take Joseph with them, and he plays in the park while they drink. When a little white girl falls off the slide and hurts herself, Joseph picks her up to comfort her, but the little girl's mother overreacts and somebody calls the RCMP (Royal Canadian Mounted Police). The rest of the story is about Joseph's family trying to protect him.

"Amusements" focuses on a Joseph, too, but the Joseph in this story is named Dirty Joe: "He got his name because he cruised the taverns at closing time, drank all the half-empties and never cared who might have left them there" (Alexie 1993, 54). When the narrator Victor and his friend Sadie find Dirty Joe passed out at a carnival, they pay a carny twenty bucks to put him on the roller coaster and let him ride all day. Later, they feel guilty for betraying their friend and their culture.

After reading "Lark Song," Chanda said Joseph was the only character in Kinsella's story that "didn't see differences. Maybe everybody needs to be 'handicapped.'" Gene thought about how the Cree and white cultures raise children. On the reservation a child is everyone's responsibility; that isn't so in his own community. Matt agreed. He witnessed a mother grabbing her "bratty" child by her hair one day in the grocery store, and as much as he wanted to say something to her, he admitted feeling uncomfortable. "We don't tell people we don't know how to raise their kids."

Gene related an incident he observed at the office-supply store where he works part-time. A father was "choke-holding" his mentally challenged son (he stopped when he saw Gene). The father told his son to wait for him while he looked at fax machines, leaving him two aisles away. When the father returned ten minutes later to find his son playing with a computer mouse, he yanked it out of his hand and began screaming at him. Gene told him to leave, that they didn't allow confrontations in the store. Gene couldn't control how this father treated his son once they left, but he didn't have to permit such behavior where he worked.

"Lark Song" does contain some stereotypical images of Native Americans: a negligent, alcoholic father and men going to town for a few beers. Some of the white characters are stereotypical, too: a woman with a gun saying she would like to "shoot herself a few wagon-burners" (Kinsella 1986, 117) and government people who poke around like "coyotes" (117), "give up easy" (118), and believe they know what's best for a member of a different culture. Even so, Matt says, "If you have read both of these stories, you would probably think that 'Lark Song' is written by a Native American author, and 'Amusements' is written by a white author."

Joseph from "Lark Song" is kind, harmless, and innocent, like Boo Radley from *To Kill a Mockingbird*. Dirty Joe from "Amusements" is corrupted by whiskey and beer. Silas unthinkingly leaves Joseph in the park; Victor purposely sells out Dirty Joe for everyone's amusement. Nikki said, "'Amusements' gives Indians the bad name they most hate. They are supposed to stick up for their culture, their family. Instead, they are getting kicks out of a horrible prank just like the whites would." Gene and Matt saw Kinsella's portrayal of Joseph as sympathetic. Their experience with white parents mistreating their children convinced them that the Cree approach to child rearing makes more sense.

Not everyone thought that a Native American author wrote "Lark Song" or that Kinsella's depiction of the Cree was positive. Their main objection was language. "This dialect sounds like a 'Me-Tarzan, you-Jane' English," Jason remarked. "Nobody talks like this anymore." Steve pointed out that Robert, a German exchange student, spoke broken English similar to that of Kinsella's characters when he first arrived in the States. A friend of mine presented this story to teachers in Montana and heard the same criticism Jason expressed from white participants at the workshop. One Native American teacher, though, claimed the dialect rang true for her.

Both stories are ripe for interpretation. I understand more each time I read them. The characters are interesting; the themes, complex; the endings, provocative. Just because a Native American author writes about his own culture doesn't guarantee a sympathetic portrayal. A white author writing outside his culture doesn't mean the characters he invents will be flat and stereotypical. Are either of these stories accurate representations? I don't know. I'm not a Native American scholar. I'm a high school teacher who's expected to help students pass proficiency tests, teach them to write, engage them with different texts and authors. I don't want to ignore texts that were not part of my own teacher training simply because I'm not as familiar with them as I am with British and Euro-American culture. Having my students read

"Lark Song" and "Amusements" strikes me as worthwhile, not only to discuss cultural representation, but because the stories themselves are so rich and rewarding.

Immersion in Cultural Themes

In addition to these stories, Amy and I used excerpts from two films to help students think further about the cultural representation of Native Americans: *Stagecoach* and *The West—One Sky Above Us*. The first was produced in 1939 and directed by John Ford. John Wayne stars as a cavalry officer in charge of a group of settlers he's transporting through "Apache country." One of his advisors is a Cheyenne Indian, about whom is said, "[He] hates Apaches worse than we do." Geronimo is named a "butcher," and an innkeeper's wife along the way, a "savage" and "squaw." (The actress portraying her is not Native American.) My students found the portrayals of Native Americans in this film so stereotypical that they were laughable. It was hard for them to take anything about the film seriously.

The second film is a documentary in which a number of Native Americans are interviewed. We learn that the myth and reality of westward expansion were two different things: although white settlers claimed their movement westward was about "progress" and "a better world," the reality was that these newcomers settled wherever they wanted without regard for whether the environment could support them. As Jason said in a free writing following the film, "They [Native Americans] were different from us in the respect that they didn't change the world to fit them, they respected nature and changed themselves to fit the world."

"Black Wampum," also by Kinsella, reinforced for students what they learned in the documentary. When Billy Jawbone accidentally kills the infant child of the white farmers who employ him, he resorts to the tradition of "black wampum"—repaying the loss he caused in kind. Over his wife's objections, he offers their own child to the Winemullers, the dead baby's parents. They accept, and Billy's wife Jean cuts both arms from the "back of the hand to the elbow" (Kinsella 1978, 111).

I supposed Kinsella had researched this tradition but couldn't corroborate that until we watched an excerpt from "One Sky Above Us." When Buffalo Bird Woman's husband died, she mourned in the "traditional way": cutting off her hair and the tip of her little finger. My students were moved by Buffalo Bird Woman's account of her mourning, but Billy and Jean Jawbone moved them as well. Reading Kinsella's stories exclusively is certainly not enough to learn about Native American culture, but excluding his stories doesn't strike me as appropriate either. When we find literature that moves students to walk in other people's shoes, we should move them—regardless from what culture that author originates.

John (Fire) Lame Deer's "Talking to the Owls and Butterflies" moves them, too—to view their own culture through the eyes of another. "Cultural deprivation" to Lame Deer is "an upper-middle-class white kid living in a split-level suburban home with a color TV." Better, he says, to walk to the outhouse from a tar-paper shack "on a clear wintry night, through mud and snow, that's one small link with nature" (Lame Deer and Erdoes 1972, 121). Lame Deer says, "You have not only altered, declawed, and malformed your winged and four-legged cousins; you have done it to yourselves" (120). Mike said, "Examining our culture from within and without helps us understand it better. We can't always see ourselves clearly, but people outside can."

Mike's comment mirrored Chanda's after we read Horace Miner's "The Body Ritual Among the Nacirema" (*American* spelled backwards). This piece sounds like an anthropological study of a primitive tribe overly concerned with appearance and hygiene. "When I found out that the story was about us, Americans, I was shocked. I reread it again and every line I read made me realize more and more about our culture." Robert, the exchange student, agreed with Chanda and added that, as a German, "It would be better to read the opinion from people all over the world about World War II than only from people from your own country. . . . When you minimize the variety of people around you, you get even more prejudiced [because you hear] the same things from the same people and you do not hear any other opinions." Lame Deer's portrayal of white culture illuminates our understanding of ourselves; Kinsella's can do the same for our understanding of Cree Indians.

Linda Cunningham, a white author, reveals an ugly side of white culture in "Business As Usual." Her poem about a drunken Native American teenager being raped by the police officer who locks her up shows Cunningham's views of her own and another culture. Although the poem's central character is "slumped in the alley . . . around an empty bottle of Jim Beam," it is the sheriff's "savage assault," not the girl's drunkenness that she criticizes as "business as usual." When we finished this poem, Micah said, "This is sick. No one should be able to do this and get away with it. She couldn't even defend herself."

Katie said, "This could be *anyone* who couldn't defend herself."

"Could this happen in any culture?" I asked.

"Yeah."

"What if the girl had been from Indian Hill (a wealthy suburb of Cincinnati), passed out on downers, and picked up by the Indian Hill police?" I asked.

"I don't think they'd dare do what the police in this poem did," Micah replied.

"Probably not," Katie agreed. "They'd be afraid of being sued."

I want students to see that some things are culture-specific. Yes, rape happens in every culture, but different contexts produce different results.

I paired Cunningham's poem with Terri Meyette's "Trading Post— Winslow, Arizona." In Meyette's poem a young girl witnesses a different kind of exploitation as tourists "buy history in a blanket" (Meyette 1988, 42). Travis remarked, "She's [Meyette's] goin' for the sympathy plea. She wants readers to feel sorry for Native Americans, but I don't feel sympathy."

"Why not?" I wondered.

"Because she's just watching."

"What if this had been written by a male author and filtered through the eyes of a male child? Would you be sympathetic then?"

"They'd probably be tradin' for a horse, and it would be for more than 'two bags of flour.' I think a male author would try to show some resistance instead of tryin' to get sympathy," Travis replied.

April objected to me even suggesting that a man could write a woman's story: "A man can walk in my heels, but he will fall trying, . . . I will never know how it is to be a father, and he will never know how it is to be a mother." As teachers, though, we want them to make that attempt, even if they do fall.

Looking at Native American culture through the eyes of poets, filmmakers, and short-story writers helped my students and me understand a culture that is foreign to most of us. Living in Cincinnati, Ohio, our paths and those of Native Americans rarely cross (if they ever do). Barbara Kingsolver *has* crossed paths with Native Americans, though. In her essay "The Spaces Between," she and her daughter tour Native American museums and reserves in Arizona. Camille, five, says that Indians are "people that lived a long time ago" (Kingsolver 1995, 147). Kingsolver wants to shake loose some of her daughter's assumptions. Visiting various Native American dwellings erases "the spaghetti-western caricature of 'Indian'" from Camille's mind.

Kingsolver connects teaching her daughter and writing novels, both of which "require the interpretation of other lives" (Kingsolver 1995, 153). Who is entitled to write about the "places where disparate points of view rub together—the spaces between" (154)? Kingsolver acknowledges that the story of some lives "have been corrupted by the privileges of race, class, and gender" (153), but she feels justified in representing the "world I can see and touch as honestly as I know how" (154), even if that world involves interpreting other cultures. This "space" is the contact zone, where voices grounded in different ideologies vie to be heard.

It is a space that used to be occupied by the voices of white storytellers (historians, novelists, artists, composers) but is now being filled by nonwhite voices who are telling different versions of the same story (or different stories altogether). These stories need to be told, and all our lives are enriched when we hear them. In this effort to share other's stories, however, we shouldn't exclude authors not of that culture; their stories, too, can enrich our lives.

Imagination and Cultural Reflection

Maxine Greene writes that "imagination . . . makes empathy possible. It is what enables us to cross the empty spaces between ourselves and those we teachers have called 'other' over the years" (Greene 1995, 3). Although we can never actually be another person, we can imagine what it would be like to be them. When people embarrass themselves in front of other people, we feel for them. We may never have embarrassed ourselves in the same way, but we have suffered embarrassment. Literature sparks our imagination. Irresponsible representations can lead to misunderstanding, but imaginative, respectful representations can help us coexist and appreciate one another. We all have to take that imaginative leap.

For the final assignment we asked students to reflect on this unit. Some students, like Gene, still found themselves questioning an author who writes about a different culture: "Legally, they can, morally I'm undecided. I can see both sides of the story. It would be very easy to offend a culture by unknowingly stereotyping them."

Others were more certain. Christy wrote, "People of all races have access to the library, so everyone gets the same information. . . . Well-written work comes from talent not from color."

Matt disagreed: "When you're little you learn to read; when you're older you read to learn. Authors are giving us information, tales, the lives of people, prejudices. Even though these novels are fiction, people adopt these ideas for their own. . . . That's why I feel it is unsafe to write about a culture that you have no experience in."

Regardless of how these students felt about cultural representation at the end of the semester, Katie and Matt's final reflections reinforce for me that this unit was important:

At the beginning of the year, I really didn't want to take this class. I thought it would be boring. I really didn't care about other cultures. And I didn't know a whole lot about mine either. Now as I sit and think about it, it's better to know. . . . The world has so many problems because of people like me who just don't care.

Katie

Matt felt the same way Katie had at the beginning of the semester:

Before this class, I wasn't interested in how other cultures lived. But the reading, writing, and discussing we have done over this semester has made me interested in what other cultures do . . . We should learn all we can about each other.

Matt

5

Silence and Sexism

TEACHING STRATEGIES
- *Four Corners*
- *Brainstorming myths*
- *Stereotypes and poetry*
- *Reading and writing personal ads*
- *Learning centers*
- *Putting characters on trial*

History	Herstory
litany	rising
of	in the smoke
bloody dates	of
	washtub
shouted	cookpot
by	witch burning
fat coaches	holocaust
at	Heartstory
good girls	
in	of childbed
white blouses	marriagebed
	sickbed
we take	deathbed
careful notes	
of pogrom, witch hunt,	so many
holocaust	sheets
	stained

enshrine
beefy heroes
in our
museum minds

telling
their stories
instead
of our own

to
pass tests
win grants
get jobs

surviving
by
memorizing
our own
exclusion

Mary Pierce Brosmer (1984)

by pleasure
and pain

then
bleached pale
and hung
in the sun
to
fade

Mystory

of women's lives
written
stitched
plaited
quilted, patched
and
painted,
and all too often,
packed away
in a
chest
without hope

Mary Pierce Brosmer (1984)

"How'd you like to go to a poetry reading Tuesday night?" Tom asked me.

It was summer, I had nothing planned Tuesday and no reason to get up early Wednesday. "Sure," I replied. "Where?"

"Arnold's, downtown. It's Cincinnati's oldest restaurant. We can have dinner first. The reading's at eight on the third floor."

And so I met Mary Pierce Brosmer. On top of French bread, Greek salad, and California wine, two floors above the bar, I met Mary—as Italian, I discovered, as Tom who'd invited me. Mary, who taught high school, wrote poetry, and raised consciousness. She raised mine.

Mary's poetry sang to me. I'd never been to a reading before. I've been to many since. Her poems were about mothers and daughters, magic and anger, censorship and abortion. All the poems she read that night were accessible, and many were politically charged. Mary was coming to voice through poetry, and her poems were helping others find their voices.

Writing poetry helped Mary personally, but it also helped her professionally: it strengthened her teaching voice. She began to challenge the traditional curriculum and introduce students to "herstory" and the story of other poets, such as Adrienne Rich, Marge Piercy, and Sylvia Plath. She asked students to read Natalie Goldberg's *Writing Down the Bones.*

As she freed herself from the shackles of a male-dominated curriculum, she freed her students, too. They began to find their voices through poetry of their own. They collected some of their best poems and produced beautiful anthologies of their work. Many of Mary's female colleagues in the English department shared her enthusiasm for libratory teaching. Unfortunately, she learned, some of her male colleagues and administrators did not. When a parent complained about this new curriculum, the support she once felt withered. Mary said that "a healthy community is one where a lot of differences can be aired," and her district wasn't the healthy place it had once been. Rather than try to heal the school district, Mary opted to heal herself.

She started a program in Cincinnati called *Women Writing for (a) Change* that helps writers find their voices, provides support for women in transition, and allows her and her colleagues to keep their own lives intact. The program has proven so popular that it has spawned a regular series of book talks, a Sunday night discussion on public radio, and a summer writing camp for girls and young women. Mary says that the school is a place where "women's words about our lives as women are encouraged and supported."

Considering "Herstory"

After hearing Mary read her poetry that night at Arnold's and meeting her afterward, I knew my own teaching would never be the same. What she said and read made too much sense. I had not critically examined my own teaching, my own curriculum, my own role in perpetuating the status quo as Mary had. Yes, I'd introduced a writing-process approach in my classroom the year before, but I was still using anthologies full of traditional British and American literature. Mary turned me on to *Tangled Vines* (Lifshin) and *Kindred* (Butler), "The Yellow Wall-Paper" (Gilman), and her own volume of poetry, *With Fine Stitches.* I hadn't considered these voices before because I hadn't heard them. Mary helped me hear. I wanted my students to hear, too.

Sometimes coincidence helps. Because the language arts curriculum was scheduled to be revised the following year, I started my own research project based on Mary's recommendations. When I finished that reading, I called her back and asked for more. She told me about a bookstore on the north side of Cincinnati called Crazy Ladies and recommended Madonna Kolbenschlag's *Kiss Sleeping Beauty Good-Bye,* which she said I could find there. Kolbenschlag's book helped me build a framework for a course I'd introduce to Lockland students the following year, a course I call Women and Men. Through popular fairy tales such as "Cinderella" and "Snow White," Kolbenschlag discusses appearance, mother-daughter relationships, family, career, liberation, and identity.

Here were themes I thought would interest students, allow them to think critically about their culture, and, at the same time, explore personally meaningful topics. One thing that strikes my students about the female characters in most of these tales is how passive they are—Sleeping Beauty in particular, whose "hibernation" lasts a hundred years before being rescued for the "meaningful" part of her life with the prince. I want students to make their own lives meaningful instead of waiting for others to give them meaning. Expressing one's thoughts and feelings is crucial to doing that.

Many adolescent girls struggle when it comes to expressing themselves in the public forum of the classroom. As Maureen Barbieri writes, "'What do you think?' is a scary question for a girl" (Barbieri 1995, 8). Not only do they worry about the consequences of speaking out (if what they say will be perceived as wrong or if their words will make someone angry), but they wonder if the person questioning them really wants to know what they think. "Many avoid conflict at all costs," Barbieri says, a phenomenon Carol Gilligan calls "silencing," or "going underground" (Gilligan 1982, 6). I use Mary Pierce Brosmer's poem "Mama" to help them recognize this phenomenon:

Mama

Working in her kitchen,
making spaghetti sauce
for the men out fishing,
I find the little wooden-handled
tool she used to cut the ravioli.

I remember her pressing it
fiercely into the yellow dough,
defining neat squares, sealing
the meat and cheese inside,

the richness always inside
threatening to explode
in the boiling broth.

I search the newly-remodeled kitchen
for some trace of her, hating the vinyl
wallpaper over the old walls,
the formica food bar replacing
the oilcloth-covered table
where she rolled the pasta.

The only thing familiar
is this tool
for crimping the edges.

I am hungry for the rich broth,
I want to be fed woman secrets,
kitchen talk. Instead, I am starved
by silence,
the silence of her death
leaving me sole woman in a family
of men: father, brothers, son
whom she fed with
the silence of her life:
crimped edges, neat squares,
hospital corners, pinched lips
holding things together.

Now it falls on me to hold things
together. She did it then so I
could be free—
or so we thought.

She hands me the tool with work-
reddened hands, the wedding band
worn thin.

Make the pasta, feed the men,
but above all, seal the edges,
hold it in.

Mary Pierce Brosmer (1983)

To help students make sense of their reading, I often ask them to freewrite upon completing a text. I've learned through writing myself that E. M. Forster was right when he wrote: "How can I know what I think until I see what I say?" Susan Hynds adds, "Through literature and writing about the roles of women and men in society, students . . . might . . . [explore] how gender expectations often keep adolescent girls silent and passive, adolescent boys macho and competitive" (Hynds 1997, 268).

Sometimes, in the act of writing, students surprise themselves with their own thinking. Writing helps them rethink first thoughts, as we see in the following excerpt from Chaunisha's freewrite about "Mama":

A young girl is being silenced in this poem. Her mother is silencing her because she doesn't know how to cook, but her mom isn't there to tell her how. But I don't believe the mother is doing it on purpose. She probably doesn't realize what she is doing. . . . But learning how to cook isn't the only thing that she was silenced about. It was also about family because it said, "Father, brothers, son whom she fed with the silence of her life". . . . Now I am starting to believe that the mother was silenced as well as the daughter.

Trying to make sense of her reading leads Chaunisha to an important realization, a realization she may not have made had she not allowed language to lead her to meaning. Reflecting upon "Mama" helps students understand the importance of speaking and listening. These are traditional objectives in mainstream curricula—to speak and listen—but what do they mean? To listen passively and repeat after me? Or to listen critically and challenge the voices that limit them? Students need to hear voices of those who have broken the silence before they can break their own. Listening to Mary Pierce Brosmer's poetry has encouraged them to speak their own truths, to find their own voice.

Silence Narratives

After reading Mary's poem, I ask students to think about a time they've been silenced. It could be a time a teacher silenced them, a peer, a boyfriend or girlfriend, a family member, a coach, or a teammate. Maybe they were silenced because of a role they assumed, as we saw in "Mama." Perhaps a "voice of authority" made them feel that their opinion didn't count, that their argument wasn't valid. Maybe their surroundings made them feel insecure to the point that they wouldn't risk exposing their views. If none of these suggestions prompt memories, they can write about a time they silenced someone else.

A number of students wrote about male-female relationships. Vicky's "Silence Speaks a Thousand Words" begins, "'What are you thinking about?' he whispered softly as his thumb rubbed the top of my hand," echoing Barbieri's words about this question and how it can make adolescent girls feel. Except for a "What?" her character does not speak for the next five double-spaced pages. She thinks but she doesn't speak. She reflects on the last ten months of this relationship and on a previous one that she'd never told her current boyfriend Sean about. The self-doubt is apparent: "Maybe he was just like Jeremy, just waiting to take advantage of my feelings to get the one thing he was after. Or what if he wasn't? What if telling him about Jeremy just pushed him away? What if he thought less of me? . . . I would have told him [Sean] but there were all of those 'what ifs.' My mother had always told me to keep my feelings inside and never let a guy know how I felt about him. . . . I had done this all my life." In the end Vicky says, "I looked away from Sean now, unable to face him. My body shook lightly as I silenced myself once again."

In her story we see Vicky considering her boyfriend's sincerity, the consequences of speaking out, the fear of pushing him away. Rather than speak, she goes underground. Writing about her relationship helps her voice her feelings to herself and her peers, even if she doesn't immediately reveal those feelings to her boyfriend.

Kelly's story "Stupidity" was similar to Vicky's in that both writers talk about a current relationship in terms of a former one. Unlike Vicky, though, Kelly wasn't able to share her writing with her peers (at least not at first). She was her own audience. When David asks her, "What's wrong, baby?" she writes, "I just shake my head over and over, as the tears stream down my face. I want to tell him what's bothering me. I want him to understand my feelings. But I can't tell him what's wrong. . . . So I just cry, wishing there was some way we could talk about it all. . . . But he told me I was stupid—over and over. He told me to quit crying. I was making a big deal out of nothing. What part did he see as 'nothing,' though? The part where Brian held me down? The part where Brian kept going even after I said no? Or the part where I cried because Brian had taken away every ounce of self-respect that I had ever had?"

I was the sole audience for Kelly's paper the day we met in peer groups. She wasn't ready to share this experience with her classmates, but she wanted her words to speak to someone. Eventually, both Vicky and Kelly submitted their pieces to a writing contest, where they each found a larger audience—much larger. Both were published as some of the best writing entered in the competition.

Attitude and Gender

Breaking their silence through writing, as Vicky and Kelly did, doesn't eliminate the sexist attitudes that silence students in the first place. In fact, when teachers ask students to speak and write honestly, those sexist attitudes will almost certainly reveal themselves, which is what happened when Travis complained that this course about gender was trivial. "The world has more important problems," he said. "Besides, sexism never killed anybody."

Travis's comment challenged me to prove that this course was not trivial, that students' consideration of the way gender shapes them is crucial to their understanding of who they are and how they relate to other people. I told Travis I didn't want to get into a lengthy discussion of his comment so early in the course, but I asked him not to forget that he'd said it, that we'd surely return to it before the semester was over.

Because he'd broached the subject, however, I decided a game of Four Corners (see Chapter 3) would help me gauge where my students stood. The four positions I asked them to consider were these:

1. Sexism is a minor problem compared to twenty years ago.
2. Sexism is a major problem.
3. Sexism in no problem at all.
4. Sexism is only a problem for feminists who make it one.

A number of my male students chose corner four. A few chose three; many—especially female students—chose the first position; a couple, though, both females, still saw sexism as a major problem. Students raise their hands and speak one at a time explaining why they think their position makes the most sense. We alternate from group to group, giving anyone who wants to speak the chance to do so (participation is typically high during this activity). Four Corners lays the groundwork for the rest of this class; the dynamics become clear, with people staking out their positions early on. Occasionally, brave students will move from their original group if they hear arguments that make more sense to them.

For homework that night I ask students to freewrite in their journals. Kevin, who'd positioned himself in the fourth corner, wrote, "Sexism is like a scab that these feminists pick and pick till it becomes infected. It's just whining." Kristin felt differently: "Two women will probably be raped as I write this response. That makes me so mad. . . . Women are discriminated against everyday. And I believe that sexism is still a major problem. As we were discussing this in class, the guys' comments were driving me crazy. . . . there will always be the ones like Paul who would never vote for a woman president."

A group of senior boys expressed feelings similar to Michael Douglas in *Falling Down*, that of the oppressed white male suffering reverse discrimination as women and nonwhites assume their jobs, win their scholarships, and receive preferential treatment. I knew this would be a difficult group. How willing would they be to examine other points of view, to consider arguments made by peers in one of the other corners? Would they ever be willing to admit that sexism can kill?

In this course I want students to realize that sexism starts in the head, and it gets there because of the culture surrounding us. Everything from fairy tales to swimsuit ads shape our attitudes about gender—who assumes certain roles, what women and men can expect from careers, how we should treat one another. If those attitudes remained in the head, I wouldn't be teaching this course. Unfortunately, they don't (see Figure 5–1). Sexist attitudes manifest themselves in sexist

Figure 5–1
The Ladder of Sexism
(Start at the bottom and work your way up.)

Assault/Extermination
- Many women who are raped ask for it by the way they dress or act.
- Men who murder their cheating wives are justified in using a "drove-me-to-it" defense.
- Governments in some countries insist a female fetus be aborted.

Physical/Monetary Discrimination
- Women pay more for cars, dry cleaning, haircuts.
- A "friendly" pinch should be taken as a compliment.
- Some jobs are for men and some are for women.
- Some governments force women to wear restrictive clothing.

Exclusion
- Women should not be admitted to military schools because they "can't cut it."
- Women are not promoted to upper management (the glass ceiling) because they can't handle the stress or will become pregnant and leave the company.
- Women should not be allowed to play golf on weekends or before noon on weekdays.
- Some clubs are for males only.
- Pub owners in some countries make women sit in the back.

Sexist Comments/Messages
- Blondes are spacey, easy (dumb blonde jokes).
- Ads show thin, beautiful women as the ideal, leading some women to anorexia/bulimia, face lifts, implants, plastic surgery, memberships in health clubs, much money spent on cosmetics, fashion.
- Men who aren't athletic, who aren't engaged in "masculine" pursuits (physical work, math/science careers, etc.) are "wimps."
- Flirtatious women who refuse sexual advances are perceived of as "icy" and "teases."
- Women who complain about sexist jokes don't have a sense of humor.
- Assertive women are "bitches."

Sexist Attitudes

- Women shouldn't work, should be barefoot and pregnant.

- Women can't do physical labor, aren't as athletic as men, are too emotional to assume important jobs (such as president), are dependent on men.

- Men are providers, are more objective, more logical, stronger, more independent than women.

- The pronoun *he* represents women as well as men.

- Such attitudes pervade the culture (in movies, stories, fairy tales, commercials, magazines, etc.).

---

behavior. For example, if a man feels superior to women, he may reveal that attitude in his speech—perhaps by using masculine nouns and pronouns to refer to all human beings or by telling "dumb blonde" jokes. In the workplace he might favor men by promoting them disproportionately or paying them more for performing the same job as a woman. In some cases he might harass a woman who resists his sexual overtures. On a date he might believe she owes him sexual favors even when she tells him no. Men who harass women sometimes become abusive—striking, raping, or (in the worst-case scenario) even killing them. Women may have sexist attitudes, too, but more men than women fill positions of power, so women have more to lose.

I have a wife and two daughters. My wife and I both teach. But what about my daughters, Amy and Kelly, who fare well now in their elementary school classrooms? What might they encounter in middle and high school as adolescent pressure exerts itself? Will they lose confidence, as do many teenage girls (Gilligan 1982; Barbieri 1995)? Will they feel excluded when—though no men are present on the basketball court—the referee tells them to "watch your man"? Will counselors steer them away from certain career paths simply because they're female? Will they make the same money on the job as their male counterparts? Will they suffer abuse and harassment because our society forgives its male perpetrators?

I make no bones about it. I have an agenda in this course. I want women and men to share the same opportunities, the same treatment, the same regard for each other's capabilities. If this course can shake loose some of the assumptions about gender that run deep in the marrow of both my male and female students' bones, then so be it. I want the literature we read, the writing we do, the activities we complete to provide different lenses through which these students can view the familiar—that which they thought they knew but had never thoroughly examined. I organize the course to make students aware that what begins as a sexist attitude can progress to discrimination, harassment, and assault. I choose readings, films, and activities that highlight this progression. Part of my pedagogy *is* this progression. In a different context students wouldn't recognize how sexism can progress.

Myths about Gender

After the game of Four Corners, I ask students to brainstorm myths about gender, common stereotypes we all hear in our daily discourse. We write the myths they generate on the board:

Women can't drive.

Women are weak; men, strong.

Men are good in math and science.

Men are handy.

Women are good in service and clerical jobs.

Men are breadwinners; women, homemakers.

Men are better athletes.

Women love babies.

Women are more sensitive.

Men don't cry.

Women are monogamous; men stray.

Women are passive; men, aggressive.

Women like to shop.

Women need to go to the bathroom in pairs.

When women say no to sex, they mean yes.

Some of these, such as the first and last ones, generate more discussion than others. "If women can't drive," Terri asks, "then why do guys pay more for car insurance than girls do?"

"I don't know about the rest of you," Alicia says, "but when I say no, I mean it!" I want students to explore these myths, to consider where they originated, to examine whether most people in our society believe them.

One of the first things we read in this class is the poem "Impressions from an Office" by Natasha Josefowitz, which shows how men and women are perceived in the workplace. The picture on his desk indicates he's a responsible family man, but the picture on her desk shows that her family will interfere with her career. The poet discusses stereotypical attitudes about male and female employees—how they react to criticism, what they do on business trips, why they're not at their desks—his, by the way, which is cluttered, revealing his capacity for hard work; hers proving she's "a disorganized scatterbrain." When he talks with coworkers, it's to discuss the "latest deal"; when she talks with coworkers, it's to spread gossip.

Students respond to these stereotypes in their journals, explaining whether they think there exists a solid basis for any of them. One of the most interesting responses was written by Travis, the same student who said, "Sexism never killed anybody." Instead of a conventional reaction, he wrote a poem that explores alternative interpretations of the same phenomenon: "He is talking with his coworkers/they must be talking about the game"; "The boss criticized him/he'll go *postal*"; "He's going on a business trip/I wonder how many one-nighters he'll have." Travis's response shows that negative stereotypes about men exist, too. I applauded his thinking, but at the same time I was fairly certain he still saw sexism (and the course) as trivial, that his poem was a form of resistance, that he wasn't going to acknowledge that women face discrimination in the workplace. But that was okay. It was early in the semester.

Writing Personal Ads

Our next reading is a newspaper article by Carol Gentry called "Stereotypes of Women Are Alive and Well." Among other things Gentry discusses an experiment conducted by researchers at the University of Portland in Oregon. They placed two personal ads in a local paper to see how many responses each would elicit; one was for a "traditional" woman, the other for a "modern" woman. Ten men responded—all for the traditional woman (Gentry 1990, 11).

I decided to have my students write personal ads of their own (see Figure 5–2). I'd publish them anonymously the following day to see if our results mirrored the study in Oregon. Here are two examples:

> I am a single, white, honest, confident, gentle, ambitious woman looking for a single, white male 17–23, outgoing, honest, responsible, loving, friendly, faithful who would enjoy traveling around the world. No games.

> SWF seeking SWM 16–18. I'm a caring person with a good heart. I enjoy the outdoors, sports, and romantic evenings. Love to have fun and am an animal lover.

The first ad was the nearest approximation to a "modern" woman, at least in terms of knowing herself and what she wants. She is

Figure 5–2
Writing Personal Ads

Write a personal ad that you might submit to *City Beat Magazine* if you were looking for Mr. or Ms. Right.

Key: S—Single   M—Male   F—Female   B—Black   W—White
N/S—Nonsmoker   N/D—Nondrinker   ISO—In search of
LTR—Long-term relationship

Example: Down-to-earth SWM, N/S, midforties, 6′ tall, 170 lb., handsome, intelligent, successful, and competent, seeking attractive, slender, adventurous, and fit SF, over 45, who enjoys running, swing dancing, traveling, camping, skiing, and movies.

Try to be honest in how you represent yourself and in what you're really looking for in Mr. or Ms. Right.

---

confident and ambitious and doesn't play games. When I passed out the ads to males in the class and had them select the woman who most appealed to them, no one selected her. The second ad was the most popular with the males in my class.

The most popular ad with my female students was this one:

> SWM, 17, seeking SF 16–19 years old. Must be somewhat attractive, under 150 pounds, no kids. I am a caring, understanding listener who can keep up a good conversation. Nonsmoker preferred.

Notice that neither of the females said anything about appearance in their ads, but this male student does. That was typical. Besides asking students to select the ad that appealed to them, I also asked the following:

> *What conclusions can you draw about the way your peers described themselves? Do you notice any differences between the women's and men's ads? Are the kinds of women men claim they want present in these ads? Are the kinds of men women want present?*

Students enjoyed writing personal ads and reading those of their peers, but the most important step was reflecting upon what they saw in their own and their peers' portrayal of themselves and each other.

Here are some of my students' answers:

> The conclusion I draw is that the men are a little more direct with what they *want*. The women tell you how they want to be *treated*.

> The difference between the men's and women's ads is that women want a faithful male and men just want someone to have fun with.

> I noticed a lot of women used words like "needs," "in need of," "looking for," while men said "must have" or "must be." In a lot of men's ads I saw a lot of things they wanted in me, then I read on to the "must be" things and that was what cut me off.

I hadn't ever asked students to do this assignment before, but now I'm glad that I did. Reflecting on what happens elsewhere is never as convincing as when it happens in your own backyard. Nikki's response, the third one, shows a student looking closely at language and drawing conclusions that reinforce what the researchers found in Oregon: many female students portray themselves as "needy," traditional women; men insist on certain qualities that "must be" present in the partner they choose. Some of my students learned about the ethical part of persuasive writing, too (writers of personal ads try to persuade someone to pick them). One female student wrote, "My peers and I seemed more confident than in real life," a comment echoed by one of her male peers: "Some of my fellow classmates gave themselves qualities that they don't have. I think the guys did this more than the girls." I was pleased to see a male student write this because many of his female peers think of him as sexist. Writing under the cover of anonymity, though, while examining the language of the ads before him, he drew a conclusion he might not admit orally in class discussion.

Slowly, some of the sexist stereotypes and attitudes that exist locally were revealing themselves, at least to some of my students. The reading I use to follow the students' personal ads is another kind of "want ad," the classic piece by Judy Syfers called "I Want a Wife." When a male friend of Syfers got divorced (and was looking for another wife), it occurred to her that she wanted a wife, too. Who wouldn't? She wanted someone who would work and send her to school, cook and clean for her, take care of the details of her social life, and fulfill her sexual needs on demand. Syfers' piece outlines the expectations many men in 1972 had (and still have today) when seeking a wife. When we finished reading, I asked students to write why they wanted a wife (or husband). Here's Kevin's:

> I want a husband who'll work all day to pay the rent. A husband to change the oil in my car. A husband who'll fix the broken chair. A husband to paint the house. A husband who will kill the spider that frightens me on the wall. And I want a husband who'll listen to my whining about needing to go on a diet. And I'll need one who'll get up at 3:00 in the morning to make sure the sound I heard wasn't a burglar.

I need a husband who will talk to the Mormons when they come
to our house. I need a husband to move all the furniture around the
house. And one who takes out the trash. My god, who wouldn't want
a husband?

Negotiation and Gender

I want to keep these students reflecting in their own backyards, and
this is clearly Kevin's reflection of the role a husband (I assume his father) plays in Kevin's household. As children get older their "backyard"
expands across the street, to the neighborhood, the school, the city
down the interstate. That's why I show them "The Fairer Sex," a report
televised on *Prime Time Live*. Chris Wallace anchors the program about
an experiment to see how a man and woman would fare in the same
marketplace as they applied for jobs, looked for cars, and had shirts
laundered. That marketplace was Cincinnati, just twelve miles south of
Lockland, where my students grow up.

The program hired two actors to play the part of newcomers to
Cincinnati trying to establish themselves. Hidden cameras followed
them and recorded their search for jobs, cars, and tee times. Though
their résumés were constructed to make them both appear qualified in
their job search, the man was immediately interviewed about a man-
agerial position, whereas the woman was interviewed for a clerical job.
Both had answered the same want ad.

When they went separately to the same car lot—a Marge Schott
dealership— the salesperson told the woman that he had to drive the
car off the lot for her, but the man was simply handed the keys. The
woman was able to negotiate a price reduction of $795 (from $9995 to
$9200), whereas the man convinced the salesperson to come down
only $500. However, the best price the woman received was still $300
more than the final price of $8900 that was quoted to the man. When
the salesperson was interviewed later about how he deals with male
and female customers, he claimed he treats them equally but admitted
that sometimes you have be "slower with women, less technical." Many
of my female students jeered when they heard that comment. To them,
the difference in treatment was clear. Many male students said later
that car salespeople try to earn the most profit they can, and just because women can't negotiate, the salesperson shouldn't be blamed for
doing his/her job well.

The woman and man each had a shirt cleaned at a local laundry.
The man paid $2.25; the woman, $3.50. When the woman tried to get
a weekend tee time at a local golf course, she was told no times were

available; the man was given two choices. A number of other situations produced similar results. When the video was over, we talked. Males rationalized the sexism they'd witnessed; females complained. But not Katie. If women can't negotiate a good car deal, then that's their fault, she said. After all they don't have to buy that car. Women need to be more aggressive, to stand up for themselves.

We do not want to think we can easily be manipulated. We don't want to believe we are pushovers. We want to control our own destinies. Becoming aware of the discrimination that surrounds her will help Katie control her own destiny, but she has to believe that discrimination exists in the first place. I couldn't convince her and neither had the video.

A month later she wrote a paper entitled "Discrimination." Every two to three weeks, students reflect on the connections they're making between different texts, between what they're reading and what they're observing—or, in Katie's case, what she's *living*. Here's one paragraph from the beginning:

> I was out looking for a car with my mom the other day when I spotted a Geo Tracker that I really liked. So we went to look at it and before we knew it, there was a salesman in our face. When we asked the price of it, the salesman quoted us $9500. (Way out of my price range.) Right then and there, I knew my chances of getting it were pretty slim. (Probably zero to none.) But, refusing to give up, I went home and started to bug my dad about it. At first he told me it was out of the question, but I bothered him some more and I finally talked him into going over and looking at it. And once again, as soon as we got there, that same salesman was right back in our face. My dad asked what they were asking for it, and believe it or not, he quoted my dad $7400. That's over $2000 less than what he quoted my mom and me. Just because my dad was male, he got a better deal. Only one day had passed, so you can't tell me the price on it dropped that much overnight. . . . My dad offered the guy $7000 for it and that's what we got it for.

Katie could be stubborn at times, but she always spoke her mind. She's like the student who wrote "no games" in her personal ad. She didn't have to admit this experience in her paper; I certainly never would have known about it otherwise. But perhaps Katie needed to admit it to herself. Yes, she is intelligent and independent, she can take care of herself, but certain factors over which she has no control do govern the way the world conducts its business. Things can change; I believe they will. I hope classes like this one will be a catalyst.

One-Page Reflections

To complete this unit, I ask students to write one-pagers, a technique I learned from Tom Romano (and one he learned from Donald Graves). As students enter my classroom, which has twenty PCs, I hand them instructions for typing their one-pagers (see Figure 5–3). I tell them about setting narrow margins, about making connections, about synthesizing the work they've done, and about recording their current thinking on the topic under discussion—in this case, sexism. They should type quickly and try to fill the page by the end of class. The first time I had students do this, they muttered, complained, and doubted they could write much in a mere fifty minutes, but their muttering and doubt was quickly replaced by clattering keys. Some students typed more than 600 words and even managed to cram them all onto one page. Even slow typists, the hunters-and-peckers, generated more words than they thought they could. I love to see them focus, concentrate, and produce. In the last couple of minutes they print their papers and pass them in as they leave for their next class. Nicole remarked later, "One-pagers show us thinking on our feet."

A male student wrote in his one-pager, "In the society we live in, it is better to be a man. That's basically what I have learned so far in this class," which I thought was an important thing for him to admit. A female student said, "Some males in this class see women as slaves to cook, clean, and then screw."

Heather addressed the complaint a number of male students expressed about women "whining":

> I know that these views start at home and are usually encouraged in school and other childhood places, but I thought women were given rights. I know a lot of people may consider this whining, but is it? Is it whining not wanting to be told I can't do something because of my gender? I don't think it is. So if I'm whining, sorry. Maybe I'll quit after I feel women and men are equal.

Paul enjoyed the Four Corners debate about sexism, which he attributed to the fact "that females feel that it is still a major problem even if it takes a microscope to find it." He betrays his own feelings in his final phrase; he's the student Kristin mentioned about never wanting to elect a female president.

Sarah was struck hardest by the video:

> When we watched the "The Fairer Sex," all of the different attitudes we had been talking about all week hit me hard because the video took place in Cincinnati. It's depressing to think that people who live in the same city as we do are as sexist as anybody else in the world. . . . It

Figure 5–3
One-Pagers

For this one-pager, I'd like you to focus on sexism and the sexist attitudes you've observed in this first unit of the class. Think about your reading and viewing, the class activities and discussions, and related experiences from outside of class.

Set your top and bottom margins to 0.5" and your right and left margins to 1". Use a 12-point typeface. Type your name, date, and title at the top, and use the rest of the page to reflect on the work you've done so far. Type quickly, revealing personal connections or observations—be specific! When you've finished, review what you've written to see if it makes sense and reflects what you really believe about sexism and sexist attitudes.

Your one-pager should be approximately 500 words, but it should not exceed one page. This is due at the end of the period, so work quickly!

---

makes it so much harder to take when you know it's happening right here at home.

Charlie complained about the pieces we'd read in class to that point:

> Many of the handouts that I have seen are mostly biased against women, which makes us men look bad. If more of the *Disclosure*-type movies would come out, I think that more women wouldn't be as against men as much. But right now I think the women are like cats waiting to pounce on anything we do or say wrong.

Charlie refers to the Demi Moore–Michael Douglas movie, based on the Michael Crichton novel, about a female executive harassing a male employee. The film stirred up considerable controversy when it debuted, because as the first major studio film about sexual harassment, it chose to depict an atypical example of harassment—a woman harassing a man. It's interesting that Charlie chose this film to support his claim that women just don't understand men—that if they realized men can be harassed, too, they wouldn't be "against men as much."

Even though students were given different lenses through which to view sexism—Four Corners, journal writing, brainstorming myths, reading a poem, analyzing personal ads, reading and writing about wives and husbands, watching and discussing a video—many held firmly to their original ideas about sexism in late twentieth-century America. I wasn't surprised. As Heather said in her one-pager, these views start at home and are reinforced in school and society. A few weeks in a high school English class isn't likely to shake loose assumptions that fit as comfortably as last summer's jeans, but at least they were beginning to hear different voices.

Sexual Harassment and Centers

Teachers need to hear different voices, too. I learned this early in my career when my instructors at the Ohio Writing Project had us read Donald Graves' *Writing: Teachers and Children at Work* (Graves 1983). Graves studied the writing process of elementary students in New Hampshire and what their teachers did to help them learn to write. Initially, I wondered why I, a high school teacher, was being asked to read a book about elementary teachers and students. As I discussed the book with my peers, I understood. The way those teachers organized their classrooms, conferred with their students, and kept track of their progress spoke to me, too. I've been learning from elementary teachers ever since.

Phoebe Ingraham used to teach kindergarten in my school district. She's the author of *Creating and Managing Learning Centers: A Thematic Approach* (Ingraham 1997). Phoebe teaches her young students early in the year how to take charge of their own learning. She sets up centers or learning stations around the classroom, each of which asks students to complete a different kind of activity. All the centers are related by theme, and each requires a different kind of intelligence—visual, auditory, or kinesthetic. Students travel in small groups from one center to another, completing each activity. Phoebe organizes the centers and facilitates students' learning, but once class begins they collaborate with their peers to get the work done.

As I learned from reading Graves' book, students' writing processes are similar whether they're in third or tenth grade. High school students could collaborate using centers, too, I reasoned, just as Phoebe's kindergarten students did; all I had to do was create the centers. To help my students understand how sexist attitudes can manifest themselves in sexist behavior, I organized seven centers that revolved around the theme of sexual harassment. I planned for each center to last approximately fifteen minutes so students could complete three centers in one class period.

The first center involved reading a photograph (see Chapter 6 of *Cultural Reflections* [Gaughan 1977] for more about this). I gave students a photo from the movie *Witness* and shared my "reading" of it so they had a model from which they could work. Their task was to write their individual reading of the photo *American Girl in Italy,* by Ruth Orkin. Taken in Florence in 1951, the photo shows a young American female walking down a sidewalk past six small groups of men who stare, whistle, and laugh as she walks by. Chanda wrote, "She looks like she's going to cry," and April added, "Women are not dogs." Matt, on the other hand, said, "If the guys didn't look at a beautiful woman, I'd question their heterosexuality." How to interpret those stares and gestures is the question, and students offered different interpretations. This center helped students begin to formulate their own definitions of sexual harassment.

The second center asked students to determine whether three scenarios are sexual harassment, a center that stimulated the most argument because what some students considered harassment was acceptable to others. The third was to write definitions of harassment, one for the workplace and one for school. Because most harassment in schools is student to student, whereas at the workplace it might be employer/employee, the different power relationship affected student definitions. In the fourth center students responded to a letter to the editor written after Clarence Thomas had been nominated to the Supreme Court. The fifth center involved role-playing one of the following roles: a male teenager who'd been accused of harassment; his lawyer; the female accuser; or the prosecutor. Students worked in pairs—the defendant and defense attorney, the plaintiff and prosecutor. Together they brainstormed questions and responses anticipating what they'd be asked in cross-examination. For the sixth center students wrote a survey about harassment they administered during homeroom the following day, asking questions such as, "What are the boundaries between joking and harassment?" and "Do you think what a person wears can promote harassment?"

For the seventh center students depicted sexual harassment using construction paper and glue sticks. They were not to use scissors but to tear the paper; the object wasn't to produce a beautiful piece of art but to use another medium to express themselves. Robert glued a line down the center of his paper that shows the border between flirtation and harassment. To the right of the line is a large hand, thumb resting atop the line, index finger poking just past it. To the left he cut out a small figure and pasted the letters "NO" to the right of her mouth. Robert said to remember that everyone's line is different.

Although Robert's depiction was a generalized view of harassment, Chanda's was more specific and personal. A large, serpentlike figure dominated the page, but in the bottom right-hand corner were two figures holding hands. When we asked Chanda what her tear-out symbolized, she told us about the night she babysat her five-year-old neighbor. On their way home from a street festival, an older man with dirty clothes and greasy hair kept staring at her. Chanda tried to read his mind. "He thinks I'm Tammy's mother so I've had sex before and am available." She said he really made her feel awkward and uncomfortable because she'd never thought of herself that way before. She hurried home with Tammy, thankful that nothing happened.

This center frustrated students at first because they'd never done anything like this before. Once students began talking and tearing, though, they created imaginative depictions that continued to made them think about harassment, even helping some like Chanda to recall and recount specific incidents from their own lives.

Reflection and Centers

All of this was preliminary to writing a paper about harassment that was more thoughtful and informed than it would have been otherwise. Most papers proved to be just that. I think the key was immersion in a topic that genuinely interested them and thinking about that topic in a variety of ways, which a centers approach allows. Even after these centers, however, some students still blamed the victim and thought women should consider the message their clothing and appearance sends, that they bring harassment upon themselves. Consider Joe's comments:

> Women go through so much more to look nice. And since they go through all of that, they are going to be a whole lot more appealing than a man with a suit on. That is one of the main reasons why women are sexually harassed.

Steve reveals his prejudices, too:

> Sometimes I think that women make the whole issue [sexual harassment] up to try to get a man that they don't like into trouble. That is not fair to the man because everyone is going to believe the crying scene at the witness stand. That is why there are so many problems at the workplace. Most males probably don't even want women to work.

As a teacher, statements such as Joe's and Steve's frustrate me, but I can't tell students what to think. I can, however, try to make them think. Granted, some women might accuse a man of a crime he didn't commit, but not the majority of women. Matt's reflection led him to reconsider the mock trial and draw a very different conclusion than Steve.

When we finished the mock trial, Matt reflected, "Jeff's attorneys were asking Kim questions like: What were you wearing? Were you rubbing on his back? Don't you think that it was leading him on? So I began to think, why will women who truly have been harassed want to come forward when they are constantly being scrutinized by men who are unwilling to accept that sexual harassment happens every day?"

Andy's writing led him to reflect on his own behavior:

When the photo *American Girl in Italy* was flashed in front of my face, I first thought the image was terrible . . . the poor woman. Her eyes were crunched up and her cheeks were puffy as if at any moment she was going to start to cry . . . Just look at her face and the way she covers her body. As if she had just been raped or abused. . . .

Now think, "Is this right?" Does she or anyone for that matter deserve what she is going through? . . .

Along with the "almost-hate" I feel for the men and the pity that I feel for the woman, I see that in some way I must hate myself. I'm sure that I have been the one leaning up against a wall with some of my buddies and saying jokingly that she "looks too good to be walking alone." Whatever I said, I know now as I probably knew back then it was wrong. But still I got a laugh from my friends. It gave us conversation. I will guarantee this, though. Not at any one time did I ever think about the feelings of the recipient. Now I try to squeeze out memories to see if she looked like the "American Girl in Italy" . . .

This picture carries not a thousand words but two. I'm sorry.

Using centers conveys certain assumptions about teaching and learning:

- that learning is a process
- that the process is messy
- that students are the center of the classroom, not teachers
- that students learn by doing
- that students make meaning by reading, writing, and talking

The disadvantages of such an approach for teachers is that creating centers requires a lot of planning, especially if each activity is to be completed in roughly the same amount of time so students can rotate simultaneously to the next center. The advantages far outweigh the disadvantages, however:

- Centers focus students' attention.
- They lead to productive, efficient use of time (students have to get right to work if they're to complete the required centers in one period).
- Centers allow movement (especially important after lunch and in a high school student's usually static routine).
- They encourage students to revise their thinking (examining an issue from many different angles affects vision).
- Centers engage students (Amy liked centers because they "got people involved" without boring them).
- Centers encourage students to take responsibility for their learning (whether they're in high school or kindergarten).

When Andy leans against his locker with a few of his buddies, making comments about or staring at girls as they walk by, his friends' voices echo his own. Calling students' attention to other voices—to the voices of their female peers, for instance—might diminish that echo effect and lead those same students to hear what Maureen Barbieri calls "sounds from the heart." Andy "knew" that staring and commenting were wrong, but it took this classroom context for him to listen to those sounds in his own heart and understand what it must be like to walk in someone else's shoes.

Assault and Gender

Our final reading for the semester is "The Murder" by John Steinbeck (1985). Steinbeck's story is about a man in rural California who discovers his "foreign" wife in bed with her cousin. The man, Jim Moore, had been on his way to a brothel in town when he circles back home after finding one of his calves had been killed. When he comes upon his wife and her cousin, he shoots the cousin, killing him instantly.

When we finish reading, I ask students to write a trial transcript with one of their peers, trying Jim for murder. In Doug and Rebecca's transcript, the defense attorney opens by saying, "Your honor, my client was enraged by the sight of his wife committing adultery with her cousin. I am here to prove that Mr. Jim Moore is not guilty, that his sudden madness resulted in a mistake. . . . Mr. Moore did what most men would have done having found their wife with another man, and I believe that the men on the jury will find that Mr. Moore was indeed following his natural instinct. He was hurt and flew off in a fit of madness. He was protecting his wife as well as his marriage." Later in their trial, Doug and Rebecca let Jim speak for himself: "I was so mad that I was going to do anything to remind her that this . . . would never happen again. She may be a Slavic girl, but her papa told her that this would not be tolerated by American men. . . . Her papa suggest I beat her, but I love the girl. So I went and I shot this man 'side her in *our* bed." The jury finds Mr. Moore not guilty.

Annie agreed that Jelka's and her cousin's behavior was unforgivable. In her paper with Carrie, she follows a line of argument similar to Doug's and Rebecca's. Carrie disagreed. Writing collaboratively gave them a chance to express their feelings, make an argument, and refute the evidence offered by their counterparts. In Carrie's opening statement, she calls Jim a savage:

> He left his wife alone day in and day out to do nothing but clean. While she was slaving at home, he was at whorehouses having his fun . . . . While he was with these whores, she needed some company.

So she relied on her cousin because she didn't know too many people in town. He was using a double standard. He had sex with several prostitutes, she only slept in the same bed with her cousin. But he took action. He brutally murdered her cousin and savagely beat his wife.

In Carrie's speech we see her late twentieth-century sensibilities temper her opening statement and affect her whole line of reasoning. At the end of the trial, instead of having the jury decide on Jim's innocence or guilt, Annie and Carrie let their readers be the jury. Those same sensibilities Carrie expresses might lead others to conclude that the argument used to acquit Moore in Steinbeck's story would certainly not acquit a man committing a similar crime today.

So I share Anna Quindlen's article "Society's Curious Math Devalues Women's Lives" (Quindlen 1994). Kenneth Peacock was not acquitted for killing his wife when he found her in bed with another man, but he did get a "mere 18 months for shooting the 31-year-old woman with a hunting rifle in a classic Drove-Me-to-It defense." The presiding judge said, "I seriously wonder how many men . . . would have the strength to walk away without inflicting some corporal punishment" (E-3).

Though their collaborative response to "The Murder" didn't require students to write in an academic voice, it did demand they analyze, interpret, synthesize, and imagine. They proposed an argument, betrayed their own biases, reached a conclusion, and kept their readers engaged. The attitudes we discussed at the beginning of the semester surfaced again when we discussed these murders at the end. Clearly, from some students' responses to these final assignments, their attitudes were similar to those they espoused early in the course. To be sure, though, I asked students to complete one final assignment.

Final Reflections

I reminded students of the comment made by Travis early in the semester, that sexism never killed anybody. By this point in the year, no one remembered who said it, and I was sure not to betray his identity. I did want them to think about how attitudes can manifest themselves as harassment, assault, even murder. Their paper was to be a reflection on the literature we'd read and their own experiences in relation to the topics we'd discussed (see Figure 5–4). April reflected personally near the end of her paper:

> I don't care what I am wearing, I never asked to get attacked. Women never want to be raped, we're scared to even go out at night. My grandmother went to Thriftway one night to pick up a couple of things. She had two bags in her hand. She heard a funny noise behind

Figure 4
Final Reflections

Early in the semester one of your peers said, "Sexism never killed anybody." I'd like you to reconsider that comment in light of the work you've done this semester. Can sexism harm a person financially, emotionally, psychologically, physically? Can sexism kill?

Begin by thinking about the work you've done in this course: Four Corners, the myths about gender, "Impressions from an Office," the personal ads, "I Want a Wife," *The Fairer Sex*, your one-pagers, your peers' responses from class discussions, the harassment centers, "You Fit Into Me" (Atwood), "How Far She Went" (Hood), *Kindred* (Butler), "A Jury of Her Peers," (Glaspell), "The Murder." (I haven't included everything, so review your papers and handouts.)

Use the literature to support your thesis. Be judicious. I don't expect you to discuss all the work you've done this semester, just that which made the most significant impact on you and your thinking and helps convey your thoughts about sexism.

Approximate length: 3–4 typed pages

I look forward to reading your papers!

---

her so she turned around and a guy in a mask ran into her, knocked her down, and took her purse. Two young men heard my grandma screaming and jumped the guy and my grandma got her purse back. That scares me. It's my grandma, not somebody doing a reenactment of "Most Wanted." That guy could have shot her. . . . As soon as I get in my car, I lock my doors before anything . . . thinking I am locking myself away from all the murders, rapists, and anyone else. I'm not.

Here are Robby's final two paragraphs:

Sexism hurts financially, emotionally, and physically. You are turned down for cars and jobs. Sexist pigs are putting you down with their stupid blonde jokes . . . Your husband that you love so much beats you. Your friend's dad rapes you. You are a girl. What can you do?

You ask, "Can sexism kill?" Take a look at the things you've seen. Ask yourself could they escalate to murder? . . . Rape turned bad, person murdered. Person takes a gun to work, shoots her coworkers for all of the sexist jokes that have been flung at her. Lady kills her husband after years of abuse. Sexism eventually turns to murder.

Some students used this final reflection as a forum for sounding off:

I would like to get a few things off my chest. (1) Men are better at athletics. (2) Men are better at math and science. (3) Women need to get back in the kitchen where they belong. (4) Women are selfish, moody beings whose only purpose in life is to make men miserable.

Thankfully, most students didn't reach these same conclusions. A case in point is Travis.

Travis discusses an "incubation" stage of sexism, a stage he sees as innocent, where the person committing the sexist behavior is not conscious of how he's being perceived. He doesn't intend to offend. With sexist jokes, Travis says the sexism is more apparent. Being excluded from an activity is the most pervasive form of sexism according to Travis, and only in the most extreme cases does physical harm occur. Travis mentions the movie *Courage Under Fire,* which we did not watch in class but that he saw as relating. In the film a soldier dies because his peers choose not to obey their lieutenant's orders. Their lieutenant is a woman. This is his final paragraph:

> At the beginning of the year, I was that student that said sexism never killed anybody. Now it is the end of the year, and I must reconsider that thought. Looking back at the stories we read, I can say that sexism can kill.

Travis didn't have to write this. I certainly didn't want to call attention to him and I didn't. When they shared their reflections aloud in class, though, Travis chose to read this paragraph to his peers. The ladder of sexism—from attitude to assault—is real. Some students, like Travis, can admit that.

Gender surely shapes students just as do place, family, and race. It can silence them, as it did Vicky and Kelly; it can color their attitudes about what is trivial and what is significant, as it did Travis and Andy. Rather than allow students to continue in silence, teachers can help free their voices. Expressing the thoughts they'd suppressed can be transformative, especially for adolescent girls. Exploring the effects of sexist language can lead students to recognize consequences they hadn't thought possible. Breaking through silence and considering sexism helps students take the first two steps, not on a ladder of sexism but on a ladder of understanding and opportunity. Teachers can help them take those steps.

6

War and Voice—Speaking Up

TEACHING STRATEGIES

- *Centers and complicity*
- *Writing about reading*
- *Writing about film and literature*
- *Imagining other perspectives*
- *Rereading and rethinking*
- *Poems in two voices*
- *Reflecting through talk shows*

> *Those who cannot remember the past are condemned to repeat it.*
> George Santayana
> (Santayana 1980)

> *I really don't care that the Jews were almost killed off.*
>
> Mick

At the end of Maurice Ogden's poem "Hangman," after a mysterious executioner has hanged all but one person in this "everytown," after being told that the hangman had come for the one who served him best, the hangman explains to the narrator, "I did no more than you let me do" (Ogden 1989, 4–5). With those words students are introduced to the central theme of this class.

I know the Holocaust is unique, that no slaughter before or after shared the calculated perversion that makes it one of the most obscene events in human history. I want students to know that. At the same time, although I recognize its uniqueness and hope such methodical murder never repeats itself, I think students can learn something from the Holocaust that can shape their own lives. "Hangman" is an important introduction to this concept. No one speaks out of fear of the hangman until, eventually, everyone is dead. I want my students to speak.

Centers and Complicity

I use a centers approach (see Chapter 5) to introduce this concept—that remaining silent in the face of evil makes the person who does nothing complicit—because I want to reinforce its importance. Using different centers that all focus on this theme helps students understand it and relate to it personally. At one center students watch the animated video that accompanies the poem "Hangman" and complete a checklist that asks them whether they agree with statements such as this one—I don't care what happens, as long as it doesn't disturb me—and to discuss the statements in light of the poem (Ogden 1989, 4–5). At the second center they listen to the song "Water's Edge" by Seven Mary Three, about someone witnessing a crime and not realizing until too late that "I should have done something"; students then sketch the scene or a related scene that reflects the same theme. At the third center students look up vocabulary that will be important throughout the semester—words such as *complicity*, *perpetrator*, and *scapegoat*.

At the fourth center students write about a time they were silent and should have spoken or about a time they wish someone would have spoken on their behalf. The fifth center revolves around *Terrible Things* by Eve Bunting, a picture book for children (Bunting 1980). The story is about evil beings that invade the forest looking for "every creature with feathers on its back." The animals without feathers sigh in relief while the birds are taken and killed. Next they come for "bushy-tailed creatures," "every creature that swims," until, eventually, only the rabbits are left.

When students have completed all the centers (they take two and one-half periods, about twenty-five minutes each), I ask them to use the round-robin responding technique (see Chapter 2) to react to the following quotes in light of the work they've done at the centers: "You are your brother's keeper" and "Mind your own business." They carry on this dialog in writing for about twenty minutes so they can see how their peers feel about the work they've all done.

Maus and the Holocaust

Although none of the centers are directly related to the Holocaust, each of them is thematically related. At this point students are ready to learn about the Holocaust itself. We begin by reading Art Spiegelman's *Maus*, the story of his father Vladek, who survived Auschwitz. *Maus* is published in two paperback volumes, *Maus I* and *Maus II* (Spiegelman 1986). Spiegelman is a cartoonist and the characters in this story are drawn as cartoons. The Jews are depicted as mice; the Germans as cats. *Maus I* begins in the late 1950s when Artie was just ten or eleven and a "rotten egg" because he was the last one to the schoolyard after falling on his skates. When his father asks him why he's crying, he explains that his friends skated away without him. Vladek stops working and replies, "Friends? Your friends? If you lock them together in a room with no food for a week . . . then you could see what it is, friends!" (6).

With that as a beginning, readers are introduced to the two main characters of *Maus*. The story is not only about Vladek growing up in prewar Poland, but also about his relationship with his grown son in Rego Park, New York. We read the book aloud in class with students taking various parts, discussing the book along the way. I tell them to pay attention to (1) Spiegelman's use of film techniques—flashbacks, flash forwards, voice-overs, and close-ups; and (2) the chapter titles— "The Sheik," "The Honeymoon," "Prisoner of War," "The Noose Tightens," "Mouse Holes," and "The Mouse Trap"; the relationship of the drawings to the text; the connections between Vladek's past and present—money, cigarette ashes, food, and clothes.

Besides being accessible to students, they find its form appealing. Most are amazed that we're reading a "comic book" in a high school English class. I must admit that *Maus* sat on my bookshelf at home for several years before I read it because I'm not usually drawn to illustrated books. I like editorial cartoons and read the Sunday comics, but I was biased against a medium that I thought would somehow cheapen the import of the Holocaust. I was wrong. Not only does *Maus* treat the experience of the Holocaust seriously, but it does so, ironically, by humanizing that experience. Although all the characters are drawn as animals, including Artie and Vladek as mice, the effect is to help readers identify with common experiences we all share: a quest for love, relationships with parents, good food, family celebrations, work, fear, and anxiety. Because *Maus I* leads up to Vladek's imprisonment in Auschwitz, which is the central story of *Maus II*, we get to know him, his wife, Anja, and her wealthy parents before they're deported. We see not only their strengths but their weaknesses: the jealousy, the petty arguments, the misunderstandings. Because part of the story occurs in Artie's present after the war, we also see a parent-child relationship to which students can relate.

When the class finishes reading *Maus*, they write about those things to which I'd asked them to pay attention when they first started the book. I add another option, which is to use a cartoon approach to comment on their reading. They can also generate their own topic as long as it relates in some way to *Maus*. I'm including excerpts from three papers that all focus on the chapter titles. As a writing teacher, I want to help students understand the importance of focusing and supporting their writing. Ninth graders often have difficulty writing about reading (as do many of us who have long since left ninth grade); I hope that by examining these excerpts, students will better understand how to support the point of their writing. I copied these passages anonymously on a one-page handout:

Writing About Reading

Point: All of the chapter titles are probably the best titles you could make up.
Support:
(a) In the chapter "The Honeymoon," Vladek and Anja had just gotten married but Anja has to go to a sanitarium and on the way they saw the first swastika. I think the chapter is called "The Honeymoon" because a honeymoon is at the beginning of a marriage, but in the book it is at the beginning of a holocaust.

Joe's point makes my students and me say "Duh." We talk about writing titles—that if authors title their chapters, they probably attempt to generate the best titles they can. Joe's first support, however, shows more thinking on his part. I'd like to see him elaborate, to include some specific passages from the book that show the irony of Poland's "honeymoon" in relation to Vladek and Anja's honeymoon. This is his second support:

(b) The next chapter is called "Prisoner of War." In this chapter Vladek becomes a prisoner of war. That is why the chapter is called "Prisoner of War."

Joe is a bright student who works in class about half the time. His comments during class discussion are provocative, his reading of different texts insightful. After reviewing this support with the class (no one knew this was from his paper), Joe raised his hand and said the writer needed to explain more about Vladek being a prisoner of war, that what is said here is just stating the obvious. Joe's paper hints at his understanding of *Maus*, but he needs to reveal more of that understanding to his readers.

The point of the second paper by Marcus is a bit more specific:

Point: The chapter titles and drawings gave us some idea as to what the chapter would be about.
Support:
(a) The title of the second chapter, "The Honeymoon," is a little more obvious [than "The Sheik"]. Because the chapter itself begins after Vladek and Anja get married, you figure that it would be about the happenings after their marriage, and it is.

(b) The title of the third chapter is certainly the most obvious. The title itself almost completely yells out what the chapter is going to be about. The title had to mean that Vladek was going to be a prisoner of war. Why else would the title be "Prisoner of War"? Anyone who had been reading the story up to that point and who has a half an ounce of sense should have been able to guess that.

Marcus was one of the most perceptive students in class. Though he weighs barely 100 pounds and his speaking voice is still high, almost squeaky, his writing voice is strong. In these excerpts, however, he restates the obvious, just as Joe had done. He isn't sharing his own interpretation of *Maus* but telling readers something they could guess without even reading the book.

Shawn's point is much more specific:

Point: Every chapter title in the book *Maus* by Art Spiegelman had a symbolic meaning and represented the six identities of Vladek, his father, during World War II: ["The Sheik," "a married man," "a Jew with no nationality," "a survivor," "a scavenger," and "a concentration camp prisoner"].
Support:
(a) The second chapter, "The Honeymoon," was about the occurrences of the war after the wedding. He was a married man, and he had to become more responsible. He had to feed the whole family. His wife bore him a son. He started a factory, and he was paying bills as the man of the house. The troubles began in this chapter as well. They were hearing rumors about Jews in Germany, about Auschwitz.

(b) The third chapter, "Prisoner of War," was about the times Vladek got captured by the Germans when they were in war. He went to the Polish army so that he can fight the Germans in the army as an equal. Later on, he got captured by the Germans. While in prison camp, he

had to live in a tent, freezing, and he had almost no food. His fellow
Poles, those who weren't Jews, got to have cabins that were heated
and got treated nicely. This is when Vladek was no longer a Pole. He
was only a Jew with no nationality.

The point of Shawn's paper does not make me say so what? As a
reader I am interested in this concept of Vladek's evolving identity.
Shawn is showing me *why* he thinks the author titled the chapters as
he did, and he supports his point with specific details from the text that
lead to a convincing conclusion. I always tell students that readers are
entitled to their own interpretations of texts, but that they must be able
to explain and support their interpretations. Of these three students,
Shawn does this most effectively. Juxtaposing these on a handout for
students is especially useful.

This was a happy coincidence for me as a writing teacher. These
three students had chosen essentially the same topic and had included
paragraphs that addressed the same chapters. I didn't know ahead of
time that I would conduct this minilesson, but after reading their papers, I realized the opportunity. I also included on this handout two excerpts from papers about the effects of the Holocaust on Vladek, both
of which used specific references to the text, including quotes that
helped the writers make their points. Reviewing this one-page handout
was useful to students for two reasons: They understood that their writing should be significant and that their support should be specific. I referred to this handout often when students wrote about reading.

Some students wrote about the connection between the drawings
and the text. They copied panels from the book and left room in their
papers to tape in the drawings so the reader didn't have to page through
the book to find the panel they were talking about (just as writers in-
corporate quotes into their papers). One student decided to write his
paper modeled after *Maus*. His first panel shows me introducing the
book and some students moaning that they have to read it. A few panels later, though, students discuss the book at their lockers, as they do
several times through the reading. I asked Jon if he and his peers really
did discuss the book outside of class, and he said yes. The final panel is
a student paper atop a desk. It says, in part, that the writer would like
to read the second book, *Maus II*. The school had purchased only two
copies of *Maus II*, because we wouldn't be reading it as a class, but I told
students they were welcome to take turns signing out the book. A
number of students, including Jon, Marcus, and Shawn, did read the
second book. Anytime students discuss their in-class work out of class,
I'm pleased. When they ask to read a book that isn't part of the class
requirements, I'm doubly pleased. You understand why I will use *Maus*
again.

Night and the Holocaust

Vladek Spiegelman's story in *Maus I* ends in 1944 just as he is entering Auschwitz, the same year Elie Wiesel and his family are deported there in *Night*. Except for a brief introduction to life in Sighet, Hungary, and Elie's life there in the ghetto, by the end of the second chapter, he is recounting the story of his survival in German concentration camps. One of the dominant themes of the class—silence—is echoed in Wiesel's Nobel Prize–winning novel. At the beginning of *Night*, those who do speak are not listened to. Moshe the Beadle says to Elie, "I wanted to come back to Sighet to tell you the story of my death. So that you could prepare yourselves while there was still time . . . And see how it is, no one will listen to me . . ." (Wiesel 1960, 5). The townspeople are skeptical of the incredible stories Moshe relates to them: "He's just trying to make us pity him. What an imagination he has!" (4) and "Poor fellow. He's gone mad" (5).

On the train to Auschwitz, Madame Schachter says,

> "Jews listen to me! I can see a fire! There are huge flames! It is a furnace!" It was as though she were possessed by an evil spirit which spoke from the depths of her being.
>
> We tried to explain it away, more to calm ourselves and to recover our own breath than to comfort her. "She must be very thirsty, poor thing! That's why she keeps talking about a fire devouring her."
>
> But it was in vain. . . . We could stand it no longer. Some of the young men forced her to sit down, tied her up, and put a gag in her mouth. Silence again. (Wiesel 1960, 23)

These passages help explain what many contemporary students have trouble understanding: Why didn't the Jews do something to protect themselves? Why didn't they fight back? How could they go quietly to their own slaughter? These excerpts suggest that the incredible stories Moshe the Beadle related were too horrific to be believed. No humans could treat other humans so cruelly. Even when they were being deported, they didn't want to believe what Madame Schachter's words foreshadowed, the ovens of Auschwitz.

Shortly after their deportation Elie witnesses the silence of the Holocaust firsthand:

> Not far from us, flames were leaping up from a ditch, gigantic flames. . . . A lorry drove up at the pit and delivered its load—little children. Babies! . . . How could it be possible for them to burn people, children, and for the world to keep silent? (Wiesel 1960, 30)

The world remaining silent relates to the centers students engaged in to open their study of the Holocaust. It also raises questions: Who knew that Jews were being systematically murdered? When did they know it? Was the United States aware of Hitler's "final solution"?

Shortly after this incident at the "pit," Elie's silence fosters his own guilt:

> A gypsy deportee was in charge of us. . . . he dealt my father such a clout that he fell to the ground . . .
>
> I did not move. What had happened to me? My father had just been struck, before my very eyes, and I had not flickered an eyelid. I had looked on and said nothing. (Wiesel 1960, 37)

War and Remembrance

During the course of our reading *Night,* I show students an excerpt from the TV miniseries *War and Remembrance,* which is based on the novel by Herman Wouk. The thirty-minute scene shows what the Germans called a "special action." Heinrich Himmler visits Auschwitz early in the war to see how the camp is carrying out the Final Solution. From the train arriving to the burying of dead Jews, the scene graphically depicts the details of the special action (when this was televised, a warning to parents accompanied this episode—Part II of *War and Remembrance*). The Germans took special pains to assure their victims that they were simply going to clean up after their long train ride before being reunited with their families. They were told to tie their shoes together, that their entire luggage was to be taken to their new quarters. Minutes later they would be dead. Himmler asks the camp commandant if they suspect what is about to happen, and he replies that's why they have the dogs (German shepherds). When their barking terrifies a little girl, one of the camp's prisoners offers her a flower. Later, when she and her mother are wheeled out in a cart to be buried (this was prior to the ovens being built to cremate the bodies), the commandant can't help but notice the girl, the flower lying atop her dead body. The students sit silently as we watch, serious and attentive.

The scene ends with Himmler promoting the commandant, telling him he's doing an excellent job under difficult wartime conditions. The commandant's wife weeps joyfully at her husband's promotion and Himmler offers their youngest daughter a flower from a vase in their living quarters. The symbolism is heavy-handed, but it nonetheless moves students and reveals the complexity of the German character. When the scene ends, students free-write. Jon wrote, "I feel that the Germans were like the dog that barked at the little girl when she and her mother were going to the disinfection. They bark at the Jews, but they are loyal and kind to their masters. . . . I just wonder if somewhere deep down inside of the Germans they cared for the Jews or realized what they were doing was wrong. How could they not? How could these men be so cruel and yet when it came to each other's families, they were like angels?"

Rosalind agreed with Jon and attempted to explain the Germans' silence: "I think some of the Germans thought what they were doing was wrong and inhumane but didn't say anything because they were scared." Marcus added that the officers didn't say anything "because they were supposed to accept the fact that the Jews had to die."

At the end of *Night*, we write about the last two sentences: "From the depths of the mirror, a corpse gazed back at me. The look in his eyes, as they stared into mine, has never left me" (Wiesel 1960, 109). I wrote,

> Gazing at his
> skeleton
> Elie pledges
> never to forget
> the night
> he's suffered,
> his mother, father,
> and sister gone
> forever,
> the corpse that
> stares back
> haunting his
> future.

I want students to remember, just as Santayana says we must, if we don't want history to repeat itself. I don't want *Night* to haunt my students, but I do want Elie's story to disturb their universe. One of the most haunting scenes is depicted on the back of the book's cover: three figures hang from ropes, straight and taut. Raphael wrote about the drawing, comparing its impact on him as a reader to a similar drawing in *Maus*. For Raphael the scene in *Night* had more impact because a small, angelic-looking child was one of the victims. "The boy was so small he was still alive when they walked past," not dying for more than half an hour. Just as the scene from *War and Remembrance* is explicit, so are many of the scenes in *Night*. In fact, they are obscene, but these obscenities are ones that I want students to read, to know, to contemplate. If they don't know this history personally—reading *Night* and watching the scene from the miniseries help them get "inside" this story—they won't abhor it as they should. Statistics such as six million Jews murdered are too enormous to understand. They need to understand the power of one, how one person's story can move them, help them empathize, even with something as unfathomable as the Holocaust.

That power is reinforced in the movie *Triumph of the Spirit,* based on the life of Greek boxer Salamo Arouch. Arouch and his family are deported to Auschwitz just as Elie's family had been. Prior to his deportation, Salamo had been a champion boxer of the Balkans. A German commander at Auschwitz recognizes him and cuts Salamo a deal. If he will fight for the officers (and win), he will receive extra rations and lighter work detail. Salamo literally fights for his life. Salamo in *Triumph* feels the sense of loss that Elie feels in *Night.* Both of them lose their fathers, but both also survive.

Writing About Film and Literature

To offer students another way to respond to literary texts, I ask them to write a story in which characters from the book and movie meet and discuss their experiences in Auschwitz (see Figure 6–1). The meeting is fictional—it might occur while the characters are alive in Auschwitz or when the war has ended—but it should be based on their understanding of the characters and their experiences. I hope writing a paper such as this one will make students like Mick (who's quoted at the beginning of this chapter) rethink their positions about not caring that most Jews were "killed off" during the war. Perhaps getting inside Elie's head, trying to imagine what he thinks about the Nazis, how he feels about losing his family, what he might say if he met Salamo, will help them empathize in ways a traditional literary analysis would not.

Most students choose Elie and Salamo as their two main characters for this assignment, but some bring their fathers together, and one student used Elie's sister, Tzipora, and Salamo's girlfriend, Allegra. One of the best papers I received begins,

> Dark cloud hovered over the small, remote island. The wind rippled the dark blue glistening ocean. Families bade farewell, tourists rushed about doing last minute shopping, and the last of the passengers boarded the huge ship.
>
> It was then that Elie Wiesel, a man of 38, witnessed a scene that stuck in his heart like 100 daggers. A few of the passengers were amusing themselves by throwing coins to the natives. The natives were literally strangling each other just to get a few coins. He turned to a woman who seemed to get a special pleasure out of the "game."
>
> "Please," he begged, "don't throw anymore money in!"
>
> "Why not?" she said. "I like to give to charity. . . ."

Chanda had chosen a scene referred to in *Night* as the setting for her story. In fact, these last two lines are part of the novel (Wiesel 1960, 95). Elie had flashed forward in his narrative because throwing coins

Figure 6–1
Writing about *Triumph* and *Night*

Imagine two characters from the movie and novel meeting either in the camp or after the war discussing their thoughts and feelings about what happened. Then write a story placing these characters into the setting, having them discuss some aspect of their experience.

1. Choose two characters:
   - Elie and Salamo
   - Elie's and Salamo's fathers
   - Allegra and Tzipora
   - two others

2. Decide on a setting:
   - the camp
   - a restaurant in Europe
   - a movie theater
   - other

3. Consider a theme:
   - loss
   - resistance
   - love
   - family
   - religion
   - survival
   - fear
   - other

4. Begin drafting your paper. How will you start? With a line of dialog? A significant detail? A description of the setting? What will your characters say to each other? What can they learn from the other person? How are they dealing/did they deal with Auschwitz? How will you conclude your story? Try to leave your reader thinking as they finish your paper.

5. Papers will be due next week. Proofread final drafts. Review the mistakes you made in the *Maus* paper and make sure you don't repeat them in this one.

to the "natives" reminded him of German workmen throwing breadcrumbs to the prisoners as they were transported between camps. A son fights his father for one of the crumbs, and before the struggle is finished, both lie dead before a fifteen-year-old Elie.

Salamo happens to be a passenger on the cruise ship in Chanda's story. He is disturbed by Elie's reaction, asks if Elie is all right, then introduces himself, and before long, they realize that each of them had survived Auschwitz. I thought Chanda's story clever in its use of a setting Elie had referred to in the novel, and so did the judges in a local writing contest. One member of the junior team dropped out several days before their pieces were due. Chanda was in ninth grade at the time but had just finished this piece for my class. I asked the two remaining juniors if they would mind Chanda filling in for the third girl, and they immediately agreed that it would be better to have three writers than two to represent them in the competition. The day of the contest a small publication including ten of the best pieces submitted that year was passed out during lunch. Six students from our school attended the program—three seniors, two juniors, and Chanda. Only one of them was published, and she was a last-minute entry. What a boost for this ninth-grade writer!

Understanding the Perpetrators

When we visit the voices from this tragic period of human history, I want students to understand the perpetrators as well as the victims. After witnessing the evil that was Nazism up to this point in the semester, they need to consider how such evil could cast its shadow over an entire country. Are the German people innately evil? students sometimes wonder. Could a similar shadow cloud their own lives? Might Neo-Nazism darken American souls the way its predecessor had Germans half a century ago? How does evil work?

In Todd Strasser's *The Wave*, which is based on an experiment conducted in a high school history class in 1969 in Palo Alto, California, Ben Ross's students react the same way many of my students do when they learn about Nazi Germany. If only ten percent of Germans were Nazis, why didn't the other ninety percent do something? Eric, one of Ross's students, says, "All I can say is, I would never let such a small minority of people rule the majority," to which his classmate Brad adds, "I wouldn't let a couple of Nazis scare me into pretending I didn't see or hear anything" (Strasser 1981, 19). So why did so many Germans avert their eyes, close their ears, refuse to speak out if so few of the German people were actually Nazis?

Ben Ross decides to conduct an experiment in which his students will become members of an organization called the Wave. They learn about the strength that comes from discipline, community, and action. They have their own symbol (just as the Nazis had the swastika) and their own salute. The experiment is to help students understand what it would've been like in 1930s Germany. The students get so caught up in the experiment that it soon spins out of the classroom and out of control. Wave members segregate themselves from non-Wave members. Friends become enemies. Boyfriends and girlfriends are torn apart. The lesson Ben Ross hoped to teach is learned all too well. Of course, my students say it could never happen here.

So I show them a film made in the early 1960s by Stanley Milgram based on his experiment "Obedience." Volunteers were paid $4.50 to become a "teacher" in an experiment ostensibly designed to study the connection between pain and learning. The "learner" in this experiment had to learn the second half of word pairs as quickly as possible. With each wrong answer, he/she was given a shock that was increased by 15-volt increments all the way up to 450 volts. The teacher receives a sample shock just to see how it feels. The learner is placed in another room, but the teacher can hear the learner's reaction each time he is shocked. At one point the learner cries out in pain and pleads for the experiment to end, but the experimenter in white lab coat insists they continue.

Although the teachers are clearly uncomfortable, fifty percent of them obey the experimenter and shock the learner right up to 450 volts. At one point the learner is no longer responsive; he doesn't complete the word pair or cry out in pain. For all the teacher knows, he could be dead. In fact, the learner had complained of a heart condition before the experiment began. In reality the teacher is the subject of the experiment and the learner does not actually receive any shock whatsoever. This experiment was the subject of much controversy because it subjected human beings to such anxiety and discomfort. Although the subjects are assured afterward that the learner is okay, that they have not caused him any harm, it must have taken them months before their guilt was assuaged.

Imagining Other Perspectives

I ask students to imagine themselves as one of the teachers who had administered shocks all the way to 450 volts. They've arrived home and are discussing their day with their spouse. Joe, who wrote about *Maus* earlier, named his characters Fred and Wilma:

Fred: He sat in this chair and his arms were held to the chair with these shocker thingeys.

Wilma: Did the guy get hurt?

Fred: He sure did sound like he was in pain. After the first few shocks, he started yelling about how he had a heart condition.

Wilma: Is that when you stopped shocking him?

Fred: No, I asked the doctor if I should stop shocking him and the doctor said, "No, it is necessary for the experiment that you do not stop."

Wilma: Did you think it was necessary?

Fred: Well, I was starting to doubt that shocking a man with a heart condition was necessary. So I stopped and asked the doctor again, and he said the same thing. By this time the fella was basically screaming and I was up to two hundred volts of electricity.

Wilma: Why didn't you just refuse to go on with the experiment?

Fred: Because I asked the doctor who would be held responsible if the feller was to get seriously hurt, and he said that he would be the one responsible.

Joe asks an important question through the voice of Wilma: Did you think it was necessary? Even though Fred answers that it wasn't, he didn't refuse to proceed with the experiment. By shifting responsibility from himself to the experimenter, he rationalizes his own role, the same way many Germans must have rationalized their own silence and complicity.

Shawn's character George says, "I wondered what if it was me who would have drawn the paper to be the 'student,' how would I feel if the 'teacher' wouldn't stop?" Later, he admits he has lost his honor, but he still finds a way to rationalize his guilt: "They have no right to test us this way, to turn human beings into guinea pigs." Nick's character says, "I felt like I was some sort of Nazi or something," but Katie tells him he was probably just following orders because he wanted the money the experiment paid. A weak rationalization, but a rationalization nonetheless. Through this writing, students begin to understand that people do have a difficult time saying no to authority, and that later, they find ways to rationalize their guilty consciences. I don't ask students to read this novel or watch this experiment to justify the silent voices during the Holocaust, but to help them understand. I want them to know, too, that each of us is vulnerable to pressure from authority, to temporarily losing our individual consciousness, to going along to get along, as my students sometimes say. It happened in Nazi Germany, it happened in Palo Alto, it happened at My Lai. It can happen here.

It did.

Shifting Terrain

In the second part of this course, we shift the terrain from war-torn Europe to a nervous United States. The film *Come See the Paradise* reorients students, changes their angle of vision, and reveals an historical slice of American pie about which most of them were unaware. A former union organizer moves from Brooklyn to California, where he meets Lily Kawamura. Jack and Lily fall in love, and despite her father's refusal to accept their love and a California law that prohibits their marriage, Jack and Lily get married in Seattle. When Pearl Harbor is bombed, non–Japanese Americans vandalize property and harass and discriminate against Japanese and Japanese-Americans. Jack and Lily's daughter isn't permitted to sit on Santa's lap shortly after the bombing. Jack is drafted, and Lily and her family are relocated to an internment camp in the desert. My students are shocked that this happened in the United States. They wonder why they'd never learned about this in any previous class.

Holocaust/Internment Comparisons

When we finish the film, students brainstorm comparisons to *Night* and *Triumph of the Spirit:*

- They had to leave their homes.
- They could only bring a few items.
- They didn't know where they were going.
- They hadn't done anything wrong.
- Many were U.S. or German citizens.
- They were deported by train.
- They lived in barracks.
- The supply of food was short.
- They were given a number.

Then we write. Christy said she used to understand why Lily's family was sent away. It was a "safety precaution. . . . The key word is *used* to believe that. . . . If they were going to throw the Japanese in camps, shouldn't they throw the Germans in camps, too? This really hit me. I am very much German. My grandfather would have been made to live in a camp if that would have happened. When you are a citizen of the United States of America, you are guaranteed all of the rights in the Constitution. I believe that this was unconstitutional and morally wrong."

To direct their attention even closer to home, we read Mitsuye Yamada's poem "Cincinnati." (Lockland is twelve miles north of the city.) I read the poem aloud and ask them to follow along:

Cincinnati

Freedom at last
in this town aimless
I walked against the rush
hour traffic
My first day
in a real city
where

no one knew me.

No one except one
hissing voice that said
dirty jap
warm spittle on my right cheek.
I turned and faced
the shop window
and my spittled face
spilled onto a hill
of books.
Words on display.

In Government Square
people criss-crossed
the street
like the spokes of
a giant wheel.

I lifted my right hand
but it would not obey me.
My other hand fumbled
for a hankie.

My tears would not
wash it. They stopped
and parted.
My hankie brushed
the forked
tears and spittle
together.
I edged toward the curb
loosened my fisthold
and the bleached laced
mother-ironed hankie blossomed in
the gutter atop teeth marked
gum wads and candy wrappers.

Everyone knew me.

Mitsuye Yamada (1994)

Rereading and Rethinking

After that initial reading, I ask them to rate their understanding of the poem from one to ten. Ten is complete comprehension: they know why Yamada chose the metaphors she did, understand every phrase and word choice. One is noncomprehension.

Then I read the poem again; this time I want them to read with pen in hand. As they listen to a second reading, they should read actively, marking up the poem, circling images that appeal to them, using question marks next to sections that confuse them, starring phrases that strike them as significant. Then they rate their understanding from one to ten a second time.

For their third reading, I tell them to read the poem silently, and when they've finished, to spend eight to ten minutes writing about it. They should write quickly, trying to make meaning, to make their understanding more concrete, to discover things they hadn't noticed at first. Then they rate their comprehension a third time. I ask them if anyone has achieved a perfect ten by this point. Rarely does anyone say they understand the poem completely.

"What questions would you ask the author that would help your understanding approach ten?" I ask them. They jot down two or three questions. In small groups they ask their questions of one another. After talking for fifteen minutes, we convene as a whole class and talk some more. Then they rate their understanding a final time. Typically, their ratings increase with each reading. Occasionally, though, someone will say they're more confused when they've finished than when they started. I quote Sheridan Blau at this point, who said in a workshop I attended that confusion represents a higher state of understanding. It was Blau who introduced me to this reading strategy, and I've used it ever since.

Students usually say poetry's stupid, which is really a code for "I don't understand it." One reason they don't understand poetry is that they rarely venture beyond one reading, and after one reading of many poems, most of us would have to admit that our comprehension is lacking. Teachers know, however, that we need to reread poems. We know that we can revise our readings. Those students who say they're more confused after multiple readings of "Cincinnati" actually understand more than they did before. They've learned that the poem is complex, that different interpretations exist. They see much more than they would have after one reading. The poem isn't "stupid," even though they don't understand everything about it. They still have questions about Government Square, the right hand not obeying, the hankie blossoming in the gutter. Writing and talking help. Nikki writes,

> I think I understood the part where she is saying she's free and it's her first time in a city. The part I don't understand is when she said everyone knew me. . . . Now it's coming clear because everyone knew she was Japanese and spit on her for it.

What's important about Nikki's writing is that right in the middle of it, she discovers what she didn't know. Nancy Sommer's research indicates that inexperienced writers believe they must know what they want to write before they write it. Experienced writers, on the other hand, write to find out what they have to say. If nothing else, Nikki realizes from this freewriting that writing can help her learn.

Jessica wrote, "The spittle stands for the burden of being Japanese. She says that she can't get it off. That's because it is impossible to be something you're not. You can't change your race."

Kandi thought:

> After she is spat on . . . and sees a reflection of herself, she wipes the spit and tears off with a hankie, and as she does they are mixed together so that her pain and other's prejudice become one and she accepts it and drops her hankie in the gutter. . . . The hankie blossomed . . . means the pain of persecuted people and prejudice continues to grow.

Some students believe Yamada uses "Government Square" as an indictment of the government for putting Japanese-Americans in internment camps. The right hand doesn't obey because that's the hand that is raised when one takes an oath or pledges allegiance, and the narrator can't pledge her loyalty to a country that denied her her freedom.

This process of working their way through a text is one of the most important learning tools students can develop. First, they make sense of the words themselves. "What is the text saying?" Then they interpret those words. "What do they mean?" Then they criticize. "Do I agree with what the author's implying?" It's similar to the process scientists employ:

- What have I observed?
- What can I hypothesize?
- How can I prove my hypothesis?

Lawyers ask the same kind of questions when they prepare an argument:

- What are the facts?
- What do the facts suggest?
- How can I make a case based on those suggestions?

Teaching students this process of reading a text is teaching them to think critically. They need to see what's on the surface, examine the data, and investigate the case. But that isn't enough. They need to look deeper, interpreting, hypothesizing, speculating. Finally, they make a case, write a paper, or prove a hypothesis.

Although I believe in reader response and am interested in every student's interpretation of a text, I want students to acknowledge that some interpretations make more sense than others. I'll never tell students their interpretations are wrong, but I will ask them to convince me. By listening to their peers interpret "Cincinnati," they begin to see that some of their interpretations have more credence than others. Whether they practice law or medicine or coach their daughter's soccer team, they'll use this process as they make arguments, diagnose patients, or decide on the best formation for twelve-year-old soccer players. They may not remember Yamada's poem years from now, but I hope they do remember this process of thinking critically.

Poems in Two Voices

Another strategy for exploring multiple perspectives is a poem in two voices such as the ones in Paul Fleischman's *I Am Phoenix: Poems For Two Voices*. The poems are written in two columns with words on the same line meant to be read together (see Figure 6–2). I share a model written by a friend, Mary Millard (Romano 104–106), in which she recounts the experiences of two Holocaust survivors. Through her poem readers see how similar these survivors' stories are and how writers make connections they may not have made otherwise. When students understand how to write such a poem, they attempt their own. I tell them they can trace the experience of two characters we've studied or make connections of their own, which is what my ninth-grade student Heather did:

WHY?

We were hurt	We were hurt
our families were killed	our families were killed
because of our beliefs	because of our beliefs
We are	We are
Jewish	
	Mormon
The year was around	The year was around
1940	
	1840
	Libourn Boggs, governor of
	Missouri
Adolf Hitler, leader of the	
Nazis,	
thought he knew it all	thought he knew it all
He wanted the perfect	He wanted the perfect
race	
	religion
We long to live in a place	
that is free	
	We live in America land of
	the free
	but how is this free?
They knocked on our doors	They knocked on our doors
We were	We were

Figure 6–2
Poems in Two Voices

Write a poem in two voices that relates to the themes and content of this
course. Your speakers could be a Jew who survived the Holocaust and a
Japanese-American who survived the camps; the narrator of "Hangman" and
a "silent" you who should have spoken; a character from *The Wave* and a
character from *Swing Kids;* or other characters who relate to the course.

Once you've chosen speakers, brainstorm as many connections as possible.
Then think about how the narrators will express their thoughts and feelings
to readers. Which lines will both characters speak? Put those words on the
same lines. Which lines will one character speak? Put those words on
different lines.

You should revise and edit when you've finished drafting. When your final
draft is complete, ask one of your peers to help you read your poem aloud to
the class. Practice so your reading is slow, smooth, and loud enough for
everyone to hear.

Make sure your poem reflects your learning about content and writing—that
means your poem should include specific details. We look forward to hearing
your poems!

deported to camps	
	asked if we believed—
	if we denied the church,
	we were set free—
	no one did
My husband was taken to	My husband was taken to
work in the fields	
	the road
	set on fire
	shot to death
My baby	My baby
was taken to the gas chambers	
	was beaten to death, but
	before he died they would
	smash his head in
My child	My child
sent to the gas chambers	
she was too weak	
	beaten but not killed
	so he could remember
I lived through it all	I lived through it all
my only question is	my only question is
WHY?	WHY?

Heather's poem taught me about Mormon history, a history I confess I did not know. Heather is Mormon and wanted to share the connection she made between the Holocaust victims and her ancestors. Seeing how the United States treated Japanese citizens during the war triggered this response in Heather and revealed to us all another ugly side of U.S. history.

Bo's poem "We Shall" is similar to Heather's in that regard. The subtitle for one voice is "KKK" and for the other, "Blacks." Marcus has FDR and Hirohito speaking from the grave as they reflect upon the decisions they made: to declare war and intern Japanese citizens; to bomb Pearl Harbor and postpone surrender until the second atomic bomb. Shawn compares Hiroshima and Pearl Harbor; Rashena, the Jews and Japanese; and Jason, Vladek Spiegelman from *Maus* and a survivor of Hiroshima.

After students finish their poems, they pair up with peers and practice reading. The next day the two of them read each poem together so we can hear the impact of their two voices as the connections they made in writing come alive for us as listeners. This form of writing helps students make connections that I'm not sure other forms of writing would. Because the impact of two voices speaking simultaneously adds power to the reading, writers have to focus on specific connections that their speakers share, right down to the words they use. What they write has to not only make sense, but also be believable. In spite of the hard work this project entails, students have fun from the initial writing to the final performance—especially the performance. Reading these poems aloud takes practice, and my students want to get the reading right. They usually do.

Speaking Up

I begin this class with Maurice Ogden's "Hangman" and end it with the film *The Power of One* (1992). Set in South Africa just prior to World War II, the movie follows P. K. from birth through prep school. When his mother becomes ill, she sends him at a young age to a boarding school in which he is the only English student. His peers are Dutch-Afrikaners, whose sympathies lean toward Germany when the war starts. P. K. is blamed for the British oppression of Afrikaners years before and treated so sadistically in one scene that he becomes a bed wetter. P. K. learns to overcome the discrimination he encounters because of his relationship with three important people: an African witch doctor, a convict who instructs him in boxing, and a professor who teaches him to play piano.

When P. K. receives a scholarship to Oxford, he must decide whether to continue his education or help his new friend, a South African boxer, teach native South Africans to read and write. This decision proves a real dilemma for P. K. Before deciding what he must do, he remembers the advice Doc, the professor, had given him years before: to find the answer in nature. P. K. hikes in the countryside to a waterfall, where a rainbow appears in the spray thrown before him and P. K. has his answer.

Unlike "Hangman," in which the individual townspeople feel helpless and afraid to speak, P. K. learns the power of one: "A waterfall begins with one drop of water." Uniting black and white, English and Afrikaner, is the answer P. K. sought. When he and his new friend witness students they taught teaching others, P. K. realizes the power of one.

Martez compared this power to Martin Luther King's. Although King died, the waterfall he started "kept flowing until this day. Once a waterfall has been created, it will never run dry." Raphael said that what he saw in the rainbow "was how the white light is like the Africans and is broken into different tribes and P. K., as the rainmaker, shows them that they are all essentially one . . . I strongly believe in the power of one."

Reflecting on the beginning of the waterfall, Katie said, "that if one person stood up and retaliated, then everyone would have the courage to. One man cannot take on a whole army, but he can take on one man. . . . In order to be heard you must speak up and let everyone know how you feel, and then you will notice that everyone else will stand up." Joe said that P.K., as the rainmaker, "brought back hope to those who were in the drought of freedom."

Nelson remembered a Gary Paulsen novel from first semester and paraphrased a quote based on memory: "In the book *Nightjohn*, he was trying to teach the slaves to read because the masters didn't want them to learn 'cause when you get to knowin' you get to wantin' and when you get to wantin' you get to wantin' to be free.' In *The Power of One* education is the key to freedom."

A Talk Show

Before students write their final reflections for the course, they assume roles in a mock talk show. In addition to a host, these "guests" appear on the show: a former Nazi guard from Auschwitz; a Japanese American who spent time in an internment camp; a survivor of Auschwitz; an African American soldier who fought for his country during the war but experienced discrimination in the 1950s' South; a German "swing kid" who opposed the Nazis; Colonel Tibbets, who dropped the bomb on Hiroshima; a neo-Nazi skinhead; an American soldier who guarded Japanese-Americans at Tule Lake; a German citizen. After students have volunteered to play these different roles, I give all the students cards to brainstorm and record questions they would like to ask the various guests. We start with the host asking everyone to introduce himself or herself and some of the questions he/she has written. Within minutes students stray from their cards as new questions occur to them when they hear various guests respond. It becomes evident that some students have not thoroughly examined the roles they're playing when they and their peers catch themselves in contradictions. This activity allows them to explore those contradictions before they write, however, so there isn't as much on the line. The talk show complicates what they've learned in ways that lead to new understanding.

For their final reflections I ask students to write a paper or to compose a portfolio that shows what they've learned. I want them to consider the course material and how it applies to them as citizens of this country. April asked a pertinent question at the end of her reflection: "The Jews had no freedom, but Hitler did. The Japanese didn't have any freedom, but the Americans did. The blacks had no freedom, but the whites did. Who has the power to take your freedom away?" April points out the possible consequences of remaining silent—that each of us could lose our freedom.

Nikki focuses on another important theme:

> "Those who cannot remember the past are condemned to repeat it." I guess the world hasn't remembered enough. They let it slip through the cracks of their memory, because it is happening again in Bosnia.

The final reflection helps students contextualize their learning to make it more meaningful. I want to share two longer student excerpts now to show the shape that meaning may take. When Annie contemplated her responsibility as an American citizen, she wrote:

> Hey, I'm only fifteen . . . but I guess at my age you really need to start thinking about what you are going to do with your life. When you get up to high school, it isn't just fun and games anymore. By the end of this decade, I'll be twenty-two years old. I guess I'd just better start thinking about my future responsibilities. So here's what I came up with.
>
> Being a female in the 1990s is a tough job. We've finally gotten our rights so we really have to start acting like we know what we are doing. So what is my responsibility? Well, this is one of the few classes that I have taken this year that I feel I have really learned anything in. I've always been against prejudice, but I never really realized exactly what the human race was capable of accomplishing. It finally hit me

after I had read *Night* by Elie Wiesel. I had never really known of the extent to the cruelty of what happened in World War II. My responsibility is to do my best to see that this shall never happen again.

Yeah, sure, you may think that one person can't really do much in a selfish world like this, but if you think like that, you obviously haven't seen *The Power of One*, a drama that really shows what one person is capable of accomplishing. But that one person has to have it in their soul to truly be able to change the world. And I hope I am one of those people.

The year after Annie completed this course, Lockland found itself in financial straits. Talk of a merger with an adjacent school district abounded. Most members of the community were against a merger because they appreciated the autonomy they had in Lockland. But autonomy costs money. Students and parents rallied to retain Lockland's independence. Annie was one of the most vocal students in that rally. She painted signs, generated a petition, collected signatures, made speeches, encouraged her friends. Annie was the drop of water. The waterfall may have trickled at first, but by the time voters were asked to approve an eighteen-mil levy, it flowed fast and furious. Lockland is still an independent school district.

Annie continued,

> In *Come See the Paradise, The Power of One*, and the book *Chernowitz* (Arrick 1981), I have encountered many prejudices. Some are a painful reminder of things that I used to do to others . . . and some are reminders of what used to happen to me.
>
> *Chernowitz* depicts a young boy who seems to always be picked on because he is Jewish. I can relate to that because some of my friends and I have picked on others because of their differences. . . . I've not only seen these prejudices in myself, but I have seen them in my peers. . . .
>
> In conclusion this has been one of the most informative classes I have taken this year. It has taught me many lessons and has sometimes made me want to cry. But all in all I think I have figured out the meaning of this class. If you don't stand up for what you feel is right, history can and *will* repeat itself.

As Annie's teacher, you can imagine how gratified I was to read her reflection. She made personal connections; she saw herself in a new light; she learned one of the most important lessons this class can impart.

Not all students learned the same lesson. Preston mentions *Night* as Annie had and *Come See the Paradise*, too. His thinking leads him in a different direction, though: "Americans were prejudiced against the Japanese because they had bombed Pearl Harbor. And, even if it's not

something to be proud of, I have to agree with them." Preston continues saying that putting the Japanese in camps was "wrong," but not for
the reasons I thought he would. "I feel that we should have sent them
all back to Japan and then dropped the bomb on them. That would
have taught them a lesson: don't screw with America!" Preston reveals
other prejudices in his reflection: that all "foreigners" should be sent
back where they belong: "If things are bad in their country, I don't give
a shit." "Forget all of this 'good neighbor' crap. The only person that
you have to look out for is YOU." If he were fighting for his country in
wartime, he would kill his enemy "no matter who they are: women,
children, the innocent, or soldiers, they ALL must die. . . . If I've learned
only one thing, it is that you have to save your own ass." Finally, in response to some Nazi victims being homosexual, Preston wrote, "I do
not like gay people. I feel that it is morally wrong for a guy to even
think about touching another guy. . . . Men should like women and
women should like men. That was the way God intended it. Otherwise
he would have put two Adam's on the Earth."

Both Annie and Preston are intelligent young adults. They were
two of my best ninth-grade writers the year I taught them. They reach
different conclusions because of different backgrounds. Their prior experiences construct different responses *despite* being immersed in the
same course content. I know this intellectually, but emotionally I'm
bothered.

I have to remember, though, that the classroom is a forum to air all
student voices, as diverse as they may be—even if I dislike or disagree
with what those voices express. This semester will be just one part of
the mix that constructs students' future identities. They'll have new experiences that confirm or challenge what they learned here. I just hope
this class plants seeds in them that someday will blossom into tolerance
and understanding.

7

Sex and Sexuality

TEACHING STRATEGIES

- *Surveying students*
- *Elaborating responses*
- *A questionnaire*
- *Literature circles*
- *Responding to student writing*
- *Final reflections*

I don't like gay people. I think they're disgusting and immoral.

Billy

I would worry about what people would say about me if I hung around with a gay guy.

Andrew

The Holocaust and Sexuality

The year after Annie and Preston took my War and the Holocaust class, I concluded the semester with M. E. Kerr's "We Might As Well All Be Strangers," a story with Holocaust connections—the narrator's Jewish grandmother experienced discrimination when she visited Nazi Germany with her roommate—but the essence of the story is the discrimination the narrator Alison experiences when she reveals she is gay. Her mother is shocked by the revelation and says to her daughter, " . . . it is not okay with me what you are!" (Kerr 1994a, 25). Alison's mom tells her not to say anything about this to her grandmother, but as it turns out, Alison's grandmother is the only person who does understand.

After a semester of seeing the horrors of hatred, of learning about the atrocities committed against a group of people because of their religion, of discovering that their own country was blameworthy, I use Kerr's story to focus students' attention on their own prejudices. Would they react the way Alison's mother does, or would they accept Alison because they've learned what it means to be rejected?

When they finished reading the story, I asked students to explain their feelings in writing. Marcus said the grandmother understood so well because she knew life is short and that it makes more sense trying to be happy instead of "trying to deny what you are." Mandie wrote, "I think that my tolerance towards people who are different has changed tremendously because I've realized now that everyone deserves a chance no matter if they're white, black, Jewish, Catholic, gay, or straight." Raphael made an interesting observation: "I think that this story shows that members of minorities that have been discriminated against are often quick to discriminate against other minorities. . . . Alison's mother, a Jew, is quick to discriminate against her daughter, a homosexual." Martez says he has no *problem* with gay people but believes "being gay is a sin."

Then there was Jordan, who slipped into my class a few minutes before homeroom the day the assignment was due.

"Mr. Gaughan?" he whispered. "I didn't get my homework typed. I did it. I just didn't type it." He pulled a folded paper from his back pocket, and from its thickness and blue ink bleeding through I could see that he'd written much more than I'd expected.

"That's okay," I told him. "Just turn it in fifth bell the way it is."

"Do you mind if I turn it in now? I don't want anyone but you to see it," he said as he handed me the paper, still folded.

"Okay." I placed his paper next to a stack of books on my desk. Jordan stood there. He seemed about to snatch the paper back but finally said, "All right. I'll see you fifth period." Then he shuffled from the room.

First-bell students were busy finishing multigenre papers, and I spent the entire period conferring with one or another of them. I forgot about Jordan's paper until second bell, when I noticed it still lying on my desk where I'd placed it. I unfolded it and began to read. I share it under a pseudonym and with Jordan's permission:

Dear Mr. Gaughan,

In many ways, I feel as if I should write this essay in letter format. . . . I need to express my own feelings to someone. This is a letter that I want you [to] show to no one. Not a soul. Not even other teachers. It is really hard for me to write what I am writing, and I feel as if I won't even turn this in. If you ever do show this [to] a future class of yours, I would want it typewritten and signed "Anonymous." I know I should have had this typed by the end of the bell today, but I was so scared someone would see me . . .

Well, all of this introduction, and I have still never mentioned the real topic of this essay. As you can see, I am still avoiding it. The fact is, I am bi- . . . I don't want you to talk to me after class if you are going to say negative things to me, or if it is against your morals. If you have an encouraging statement, something to help me instead of demoralize me, then please do. I need people to talk with.

I feel as if I am confessing to a crime. I guess society raises us that way . . . I really wish people would judge me for who I am instead of who I like, but I have to realize I am in the real world.

As I am continuing to write this, it is getting easier to express myself. I still can't believe I am telling you, and I know I could regret this. The only reason I am actually saying this to you right now, handwritten, is because I am taking a major step in my own life. In all of my lifetime, I have only told two people, and they are still my best friends.

I know through all of this writing, I still haven't mentioned war and the Holocaust nor the short story I read, but then, if I am able to come out and tell you, then your class must have helped to encourage me to do so. . . . "A waterfall begins with a single drop." I have to actually thank you for your "drop," for you may have changed many lives other than mine. Your class has encouraged me to stand up for who I am. Telling you through this letter is the first step. . . .

I can relate to all the prejudices mentioned in this class. I would have burned in Auschwitz just because I am "different." I can see why the girl's grandmother was sympathetic and not the mother . . . The grandmother knew how it felt to be a victim of prejudice . . . Her mother however feels pain because she . . . wanted . . . a "normal" child. But there is no "normal" . . .

Well, I am not going to go on, for I could write a whole book just displaying my feelings. And if you read up to here, I thank you for being patient and giving me a chance to hear "my voice." I have to also thank you because my life has changed with your class, and it will help me in the future. Thanks again.

Your student,
Anonymous

Needless to say, the letter was the most important piece of writing I received that Friday in May, indeed one of the most important pieces of student work I ever received. It is passionate; it is personal; it is honest. It connects course content with personal experience. I share it not to boost my esteem, but because it is a prime example of personal writing in social contexts. The most important writing I did that day immediately followed my reading of Jordan's paper.

I invited him to talk to me; I told him I admired him, that I recognized the risk he'd taken. I said his life would present challenges that I'd never known. I think now of Matthew Wayne Shepard, the gay student from the University of Wyoming, who was beaten and left for dead. I feel more certain now than ever that classes like this one are important in preventing future beatings and murders. I wished Jordan luck.

I don't think he would have written this letter in another classroom context. Although he took a risk here, the risk was calculated. He and his peers saw how prejudice starts in speech and ends in murder. He saw a progression from the Holocaust in Europe to internment in America. He saw a British student beaten in South Africa and a gay teenager rejected by her mother. He knew that his teacher felt all of it was wrong. He took a chance.

So I decided to take a chance, too. Instead of using just one short story at the end of a semester, as I did in my War and the Holocaust class, I created a unit in which students would explore their feelings about sex and sexuality in greater depth.

Surveying Students

I began by asking my juniors and seniors three questions. The first was to explain their feelings about sex in a relationship and to keep their responses PG-13: What kind of relationship is necessary for sex to be part of it? One male student said sex is about "companionship," but another said a relationship is unnecessary, that "you could just go pick up a girl at a club or bar." One of his friends echoed this comment: "It takes a couple weeks until you can be sure you want to stay with this partner, but if you just want sex it only takes a few minutes."

Most female students felt differently: "You should do it because you care for the person . . . not just for a fling or to 'experiment.'" Another said, "Don't give freebies," and a third added that love and maturity should be part of a relationship before sex. A fourth female student said that many young people are "used and then left."

The next question I asked was, Do males and females feel the same way about sex? A male student admitted that guys are the ones "pushing to have sex," and one of his female peers agreed: "Guys want it more." A male student summed it up this way: "Girls view sex as a way to get love, and guys view love as a way to get sex." Most of his classmates agreed his statement fairly represented their views. The most humorous response came from a female who said, "A girl wants to cuddle afterwards, a guy wants a bagel," a response that drew laughter but that echoed the preceding comment.

The final question evoked the most passionate responses: Would your answer to the first question change if I had said, "Explain your feelings about sex in a gay relationship"? One student wrote, "Homo sex is sick and must be exterminated. If it wasn't for the damn liberal Democrats, we wouldn't even be talking about this." A peer said, "You will never be able to prove to me that from birth you have wanted nothing but your own sex. No, no, no, that just doesn't happen." Both of those responses came from males. Most, but not all, females disagreed: "People have a right to be with whomever will make them happy" and "If it makes you happy, go for it" were common responses. One female, however, voiced a familiar sentiment to condemn homosexuality: "It's against the Bible." She wasn't the only student alluding to the Bible, as evidenced in this response from a male student: "The Bible said that the man who murders is more likely to gain admittance to heaven than the man who judges; if it is a sin to be gay, God will take care of it, not me."

Elaborating Responses

These responses were adequate to start discussion, to survey the terrain of student views, but they only hinted at what lay beneath the surface. Students' first opportunity to elaborate on their responses followed this discussion. They saw how their classmates responded to the same questions and had an idea how their peers viewed relationships with the opposite (and the same) sex. I asked them to explain the feelings behind their responses and to react to what they heard their peers say. Jason titled his paper "The Last Cowboy":

> I am a guy. I have all the required parts to be a guy. All except one it seems to me now. Everyday I hear about how bad we are, how much we hurt them. The last time I checked, I didn't look like a giant anal orifice in the mirror. I was a human being, or at least as close as one could expect.
>
> I sit in art class sculpting pieces of primitive pottery out of wet clay and I overhear girls speaking of how all guys are assholes, all guys are pricks. "MEN!!" they say, "men." It hurts to hear this. Not as much because I am forced unwillingly into this dreaded category, but that

someone has injured them so badly that they have lost all apparent hope in MANkind.

I do not know why some guys do the things they do. I cannot even begin to fathom how someone can beat his wife into a mass of blood and tears and pain. Perhaps I am flawed because these violent emotions seem to evade me. . . .

I love my girlfriend. I would give her the world if I could. Yet, I cannot. Like I said, I am just a guy. I don't have a billion dollars to buy her her own island in the Caribbean; I do not have a powerful sports car to escort her through the streets of Beverly Hills. I do not own a mansion in the country with chefs and maids and butlers to wait on her every whim. But I have me. I can give her my heart and I can promise her my devotion. That, to me, would be worth more than any mansion, sports car, or island.

The other day I was driving down Chester Road on my way to work in my red "Hillbilly Hauler" pickup truck. I had the radio set to Q102 and when I was stopped at a traffic light, they began to play "Where Have All the Cowboys Gone?" by Paula Cole. My stereo is definitely not one to look at twice but nonetheless, it carried across the valid message hidden in that woman's words.

She asks, "Where is my John Wayne, where is my Prairie John, where is my Lonely Ranger, where have all the cowboys gone?" I was stunned by these words until horns began to blare behind me signaling me to get the hell out of the way. And I realized what I wanted to be. Not some jackass riding around on a horse in the country, but a modern-day knight, if you will. A regular human being who still lives by the basic code of chivalry. . . .

After reading this, you may not see how I feel about sex in a relationship. If so, it is because you aren't paying attention. . . . My feelings on sex are simple: if you love them and mean it, then rock on. If it's for a good time or just the penile pleasure you get from boning a pretty girl, you make me sick. It's because of people like you that nobody even hopes for the cowboy anymore.

I pledge to be the cowboy. Even if I am the last.

Jason sees himself as a "nice guy" who knows how to treat a girl "right," but who doesn't "get much play." Unfortunately, he thinks, the good-looking "assholes" who mistreat women get more dates than "nice guys." This paper is his attempt to set things straight, to show his female peers that not all guys are jerks. When I've read his paper aloud to high school and college classes (anonymously but with his permission), most females sigh in unison when I read the last line. I take that to mean the paper moved them, that the writer made his mark. But is the writing honest? Two weeks later when discussing sexual harassment, Jason joked, in the middle of class, that he never knew "harass" was one word. In fact, Jason frequently made sexist comments in and out of class.

Perhaps that isn't surprising. The man and woman he describes in "The Last Cowboy" exemplify a traditional woman and man. The woman is passive; the man, chivalrous. The woman, dependent; the man, independent. The woman, controlled; the man, controlling. Although many females listening to this paper sigh at the end, is this really the kind of man they want?

Three Texts and Heterosexuality

The three texts we read next help students explore what they want in more depth. "The Sexes" by Dorothy Parker (1976) and the songs "It's My Party" and "Judy's Turn to Cry" sung by Lesley Gore(1963a, b), are each about romantic triangles. In "The Sexes," a young man and woman argue about cigarettes, boredom, and stupidity, leaving the reader to wonder what happened before the present scene to produce such chilly rhetoric. Readers discover later in the story that the young man had spoken to a "pretty" woman named Florence Leaming at a party the night before, upsetting the young woman—who, according to the man, had ignored him the entire evening. In the end, after a saccharine string of flattering phrases, they make up with one another, the young woman saying, "Ow, my new pearl beads! Wait a second till I take them off. There!" (Parker 1976, 37).

In the first Lesley Gore song, the female narrator is upset when a guy named Johnny runs off with "a Judy," who returns wearing his ring. Because it's the narrator's party, she can cry if she wants to. In the second song, the narrator kisses a different guy at another party, and Johnny punches the guy to claim his former girlfriend. Now "it's Judy's turn to cry." In both cases a young man finds himself between two young women: is he blameworthy or victim?

Though these are nontraditional texts, students can write traditional analysis papers in which they compare and contrast similar situations. One female student wrote that guys string girls along just for the sex and then dump them when they find "something better." One day they see their ex- on the street with another girl and don't know what to do. This student said they should "ruin his game" right then instead of trying to get revenge on the other girl, as the narrator does in "Judy's Turn to Cry."

A male student tried to justify Johnny's actions by saying it's natural for males to have as many sexual partners as possible. "It is something in our genes that's been around since our monkey days." One female student said that Johnny is possessive, that he thought of the narrator as his "territory," and that the other guy was "trespassing." A male student saw Judy as the culprit, saying that she was jealous and "toying with Johnny's emotions" because he is caught in the middle and will end up walking away with "scars on his heart."

Most students placed blame on the young woman in "The Sexes" for not speaking her mind when she and the young man were talking the following day and for ignoring him the night before at the party. Most males and females alike, however, considered Johnny more blameworthy than the young man from "The Sexes." These texts gave students an opportunity to write "academic" papers about nontraditional texts, texts they found appealing and interesting. In their papers they analyzed the texts, citing passages that supported their thesis. The story and songs acted as catalysts to explore male-female relationships and to spark discussion about what motivates males and females. Most students agreed that these characters veil their feelings instead of communicating frankly. I hoped that reading and writing about them would prepare students to communicate frankly themselves about same-gender relationships.

Sexuality and Identity

I use Barbara Kingsolver's short story "Rose-Johnny" to bridge this shift in perspective (Kingsolver 1989). Rose-Johnny is the object of a small Southern town's gossip in the 1950s because the townspeople believe her to be "Lebanese" (their mistake): she wears her hair short and dresses like a man. The narrator, Georgeann, hears rumors about how "manly" Rose-Johnny is, but when she works for her in a feed store, she sees that her new friend is gentle and kind. She learns that her boss's name used to be Rose, but when her half-brother is murdered because he's mulatto, her mother tells her she has to be both Rose and Johnny. The story shows how gender and sexuality shape identity. When Georgeann's sister Mary-Etta is beaten late in the story, the narrator changes her name to George-Etta and cuts her doll's hair to remind her of Rose-Johnny.

Travis wrote in a short-answer quiz over the story that "your whole identity can be created or destroyed depending on your sexual preferences." Georgeann's classmates disliked her because she "was friends with a lesbian." Jenilee said that Rose-Johnny's mother was targeted, too, because she challenged the sexual mores of the town: "Rose-Johnny's mother took the man she loved and had offspring even though he was black. She went against the morals of the town and paid the consequences." Even though the story suggests that Rose-Johnny is not gay, some student readers reacted as the townspeople did. Rose-Johnny clipped her hair short, wore work boots, and worked in the feed store, so she must be gay. Like some of the men in the town, they didn't think Georgeann should work there because of the negative influence Rose-Johnny might have on her.

A Questionnaire

Once students have crossed the bridge created by Kingsolver's short story, we deal directly with homosexuality. I give them a survey called The Language of Sex: The Heterosexual Questionnaire (Rochlin 1992). The eighteen questions are rewritten for heterosexuals but are commonly asked of homosexuals.

1. What do you think caused your heterosexuality?
2. When and how did you decide you were a heterosexual?

I ask students to read the questions and to respond in writing about how the questions made them feel. William wrote, "These questions are silly. I think they are trying to get us to think about maybe turning gay." Misty reacted differently: "These questions bothered me very much. They were more of an interrogation than a survey." I agree with William that the questions are silly and with Misty that they are interrogatory. I want students to understand how invasive such questions can be.

Literature Circles

To really help them understand that concept, though, they need more than a discussion of eighteen questions. For their next assignment (see Figure 7–1), students choose one of three books to share in literature circles (Daniels and Bizar 1998): *Annie on My Mind* by Nancy Garden (1982), *Deliver Us From Evie* by M. E. Kerr (1994a), and *The Drowning of Stephan Jones* by Bette Greene (1991). *The Drowning of Stephan Jones* is about two gay men who relocate to a small town in Arkansas, only to discover that they can't escape discrimination there either. The characters in this novel are mostly flat except for the female narrator, whose relationship with Andy is complicated when she realizes how bigoted he is. The novel is good for discussing heterosexuals' use of the Bible to justify their prejudices. *Deliver Us From Evie* is about a witty young woman who is comfortable with her homosexuality and her relationship with Patsy Duff, daughter of one of the most prominent families in town. When Patsy's father protests his daughter's relationship with Evie, Patsy and Evie leave town to begin a new life. *Annie on My Mind* is about two teenage girls who meet in New York and fall in love. Later in the novel they housesit for two of Liza's teachers and discover the

Figure 7–1
Lit Circles

With the other members of your group, choose one of the following books to read:

- *Annie on My Mind*
- *Deliver Us From Evie*
- *The Drowning of Stephan Jones*

You will have periodic discussions about your novel, and each of you will be responsible for preparing a different role each time you meet:

- Discussion director: Write 5–10 questions about this section of the book that will generate discussion among your peers—don't write simple recall or "yes/no" questions.
- Literary luminary: Choose two or three important passages from this section, write down the first and last words of the quote ("First words . . . last words"), the page number, and why you think they are significant.
- Connector: Find at least five connections between this reading and other readings, movies, observations, experiences, etc., that relate to the book—be prepared to discuss them in class.
- Illustrator: Sketch something from this portion of the book that you find significant—think about a symbolic drawing that will generate discussion.

You will continue to meet with the same group and prepare for discussions in the same way. Be sure you all assume each role once during the reading of your book. You will be quizzed over your book periodically; be sure to average reading 15–20 pages per day.

teachers are also gay. Unlike *Evie* and *Stephan*, which are narrated by heterosexual characters, *Annie*'s narrator is gay. The book is well written and the best of the three at helping heterosexual readers walk in someone else's shoes.

Students assume one of four different roles when they meet in lit circles with their peers reading the same book: illustrator, discussion director, connector, and literary luminary. The illustrator depicts something significant; the discussion director asks questions that require more than yes/no answers; the connector relates the novel to other texts, observations, or experiences: the literary luminary finds passages worthy of a second look. The point of assuming these roles is to help students direct their own discussion of the book, to show their peers a different way to read the novel.

Christy's first question as discussion director for *Stephan Jones* is the kind of question that provokes thoughtful conversation: "Do you believe that child molesters, pornographers, and homosexuals should be grouped together as they are on page two of the novel?" She also asked, "If your crush disagreed with one of your principles, would you drop it or continue to fight for what you believed?" I'll use these questions as models the next time my students participate in lit circles because they're such good examples. The first helps students distinguish behaviors; the second, decides what they'd sacrifice for a relationship.

As literary luminary, Amanda chose two paragraphs from *Stephan Jones* to discuss religion and homosexuality:

> *"Compassion!"* shrieked the minister . . . "There is *no* compassion for sodomites! . . . Read your Bible, because there it is written that the one sin that can never be forgiven is the sin of blasphemy."
>
> "Blasphemy, is it?" taunted Frank . . . Well, *Reverend*, it so happens that I may not have read the Bible, but I have read my history and that's why I can tell you this: If Stephan is guilty of blasphemy, why then, he's in damn good company because both the Bible and history teach of two men who have been tried, convicted, and finally put to death for the crime of blasphemy. Maybe you know them? Their names were Socrates and Jesus Christ." (Greene 1991, 109–110)

Amanda said she chose these paragraphs because she thought they showed what was important to the Reverend. "Reverend Wheelright does not preach or live what's in the Bible. . . . he thinks that if you aren't like him then you'll go to hell. He hates everyone but himself." Choosing passages such as this one focuses students' attention on the novel's central dilemma: whether to love thy neighbor as thyself or to use the Old Testament to justify prejudice. Christy resolved that dilemma in her own mind when she wrote, "Love and respect are the basis of all religions. If you can't love or respect people for being themselves, then you aren't very religious yourself."

Students connected the book to their own relationships, to acquaintances they knew at work, to prejudices they've observed at school. As illustrators, they drew different depictions of the verbal and physical abuse suffered by Stephan and Frank, scales with "love" on one side and "hate" on the other. I grade students' preparation for lit circles to nudge them so they'll have thoughtful discussions. As in any peer group work, some groups function better than others. What I like about using lit circles for this unit is that all students focus on the same issue but with different books. Often, fast readers ask me if they can read the second or third novel, for which I give them extra credit.

For those students who do not read more than one book, I ask their peers to prepare an oral presentation to give them an idea of what the other novels are about. Some groups use talk-show formats; others conduct trials. Holly, Dawn, Mike, Chrissy, and Sarah held a hearing to discuss the fate of the two gay teachers and Liza in *Annie On My Mind*.

They typed a transcript of the hearing, summarized the plot to that point of the book, and role-played the various parts. Their hearing revolved around the climax and how the events that transpired there might be interpreted. The rest of the class became the board of trustees at the school and decided what should be done with Liza and the teachers when the hearing concluded.

Rachle, Molly, Angie, and Nicole used a variation of Four Corners to discuss *The Drowning of Stephan Jones*. If, after hearing about Stephan's drowning, students believed Andy was guilty of manslaughter, they chose one corner. If they thought his crime was murder, they chose the opposite corner. Each of these strategies got the class involved, provoked further discussion, and hinted at what the other books were about.

The group presentations helped me gauge general reactions to the three books, but I also was interested in how students felt individually. I asked them to write one-pagers (see Chapter 5) the day after presentations were finished and told them I wanted them to write honestly. As long as they wrote specifically about their book and generated close to a page of writing, they received full credit. I'm fairly certain Billy took me at my word:

> I pretty much figured out Evie was a lesbian when they first described her. I just want to know what the hell Patsy was thinking. Here is a hot chick that has everything. Yet she gives it all up to be with a girl that looks like a man, who works on a farm, who basically has nothing. She just didn't meet the right man. Me. I could change her ways.

Billy's writing reveals his assumptions about homosexuality: that it is a choice, that a relationship with the "right" heterosexual can "cure" a gay "illness." Most students were not as upset by the novels as Billy, but some, like Julie and Sarah, said reading about gay characters shook them from their "comfort zone." Sarah wrote,

> It made me feel a little uncomfortable at first when I read parts about Liza and Annie being sexually involved . . . but after I got so far into the book, I started to feel sorry for [them]. . . . Liza and Annie loved each other and they were punished for that. That's completely wrong!

Annie railed against the same kind of discrimination in her response to *The Drowning of Stephan Jones*. She said the novel shows that "the justice system does not serve all Americans," because Andy's sentence for his involvement in Stephan's drowning amounted to no more than a slap on the wrist. Rachle said she'd never given much thought to homosexuality before because it was something that didn't affect her. After reading *Stephan Jones*, however, she wrote, "This book, shown from the point of view of a teenage girl who is not homosexual but who dates a homophobic boy, helped me to realize that it could touch anyone."

Many students related the novels to their own relationships. Holly said she knew from experience how Annie and Liza felt: "It was almost as if they were talking about me and my life." Shannon said she got caught with her boyfriend in circumstances similar to Annie and Liza getting caught by their teacher. Carrie said she could relate to Evie and Patsy staying together despite the townspeople's objections because she stayed together with her boyfriend even though a lot of her friends "couldn't imagine someone like me going out with someone like him."

Responding to Student Writing

I found these papers easy ones to respond to. For example, William wrote, "If Evie had been straight, Parr could have followed his dream and gone through school pretty much without embarrassment. If it had been me, I would have disowned my sister and acted like I had never even had one." I wrote back: "What about Evie's dreams? Could you really disown her?" Because I really wanted to know if William were exaggerating and because I wanted him to think further about who's entitled to dream, I asked students to respond to my responses. William wrote back to me, "If her dream was to be gay, then she didn't deserve for her dreams to come true, and yes, I could really disown my sister. I disowned my cousin for what she did to me and my family." I didn't think it my business to find out what his cousin had done, but I did address the first part of his response: "Maybe Evie's dream was to find someone to love."

Brian had written, "There wasn't one person who wanted Patsy with Evie," to which I responded, "What about the two of them? Aren't they most important? No one wanted Romeo and Juliet together either." Brian wrote back, "Is it worth giving up your family and having them in a feud not only with you but with another family? I don't think so. Maybe it will change when I get older." I like how Brian leaves the door open, admitting his feelings may change. Teachers rarely know the effect their classes might have because most of it is felt after students depart. Some, like Brian, admit that possibility.

Final Reflections

Besides these dialogs, which engaged my students and me, this unit was satisfying for other reasons. A number of students had their best reading experiences with these novels. Joey said, "This [*Annie*] was the most interesting book I ever read." Jimmy wrote, "I was surprised to find myself actually reading a book [*Evie*] to find out what was going to happen next." Angie just "had to read" *Annie* after *Stephan* because she wanted to understand homosexuality from the point of view of "both sexes." And Chris, who barely passed the class with a D, wrote, "By the middle of the book [*Evie*], I was reading whenever I had a chance. The book even found its way home with me a few days a week."

Most gratifying, though, was a response from Mike. Mike was a wrestler, a nice kid with conservative—sometimes radical—views. He hated talking about tolerance in school. Books about racial differences irritated him. So when I read the beginning of his response to *Annie On My Mind*, I wasn't surprised:

> "Three books to choose from and all three are about faggots." That was my first reaction to the three books we had to choose from. I chose *Annie On My Mind* because I thought that I sure didn't want to read about the guys.

What followed, though, was a surprise:

> The book wasn't at all what I thought it would be about. . . . I figured it would be about some sick lesbian lovers who were constantly flee-ing some kind of persecution.
> This novel wasn't about that at all, though. It was about people. Not gay people either. It was about normal people finding their true identity in a world that doesn't accept them because they have a dif-ferent sexual preference than you or me.
> The novel opened my eyes up to a whole new concept that I had never thought about when it came to homosexuality. Love.

Jordan's letter at the beginning of this chapter was, as I said, one of the most important pieces of student writing I ever received. It still is. But this piece from Mike is just as important. He examined his as-sumptions about homosexuality and admitted them; he revealed his expectations for the novel he was about to read, even though they were negative; he completed the reading despite those expectations; he learned something about himself and others. Mike ended his paper by writing,

> I guess this book is another example of how this class makes me think twice about some of my attitudes on certain societal issues I felt so strongly about. All year long my opinion keeps being changed.

When students had completed their written responses, I reminded them of the way prejudice works like a ladder, beginning in speech, ending in extermination. I asked them to consider this unit in terms of that ladder. Andreia said, "In *The Drowning of Stephan Jones*, Andy moved slowly up the ladder. First, in the store he calls Frank and Stephan names. Then they have to leave, which would be avoiding seeing them. He moves up to discrimination and physical attack when he hits him and smashes a pizza in Stephan's face. Finally, Andy reaches the final rung, extermination, when Stephan is thrown over the bridge."

I asked students to place themselves on the ladder. Most said they are on the first rung of speech. They admit using slurs like "fag, queer, lezzie, or dyke." A few said they avoid homosexuals, and one confessed he was in between avoidance and discrimination. One student went further: "I would put myself on the fourth step. Like I said, if a gay guy hit on me, I would beat the heck out of him." A few students remembered the gay student who'd been beaten to death in Wyoming, though they couldn't recall his name. Though no one claimed to be on this fifth rung, anyone on the ladder could end up there. What seems innocent or funny at first can turn violent later.

To finish this unit, we read one more story by Leslea Newman called "Right Off the Bat," which begins, "My mother is a lesbian" (Newman 1999, 120). The narrator wants readers to know that fact right off the bat, because she's learned the importance of being honest. When one of her friends stops talking to her because her mother's a "dyke," Ronnie resents her mother's overt behavior. By the time the story's finished, however, she's learned to accept her mother for who she is and asks the reader if they can accept her: "Do you think your mom will let us be friends?" (126). This story was the catalyst for a final paper.

Apparently, Kristi was one of the two people besides me to whom Jordan, from the beginning of this chapter, had written about his bisexuality. When she received his letter, she said, "I could feel my face transforming, clammy and crimson. I was astonished. I would have never suspected *him* of being gay. He never flipped his hand in *that* way. He never had that *funny* walk and didn't talk with a high-pitched 'girly' voice. Soon I realized that I was being stereotypical and wasn't being supportive. . . . Believe it or not, I went to the dictionary to find the meaning of 'friend': *one who supports or sympathizes*. I knew at that moment that I couldn't shut him out. I was still going to be his friend. It would have been stupid if I wasn't."

Kristi concludes her paper by saying she would be a friend to Ronnie from "Right Off the Bat" because "she seems very smart and opinionated. That sounds like my kind of friend. Someone I can argue with! Now that you know where I stand . . . do you still want to be my friend?"

Unlike Andrew, who's quoted at the beginning of this chapter, Kristi doesn't worry about what people will think of her because of whom she chooses to befriend. If students can't be friends with some-one who's gay, I hope they will at least learn what another Christy did:

> This unit has taught me a lot more than just to accept gays and les-bians. It has taught me about being tolerant of people who are differ-ent than me. On the ladder of love and understanding, tolerance is an important step. If only more people could reach that rung.

8

Censorship and Faith

TEACHING STRATEGIES
- *Defending texts*
- *Considering texts*
- *Constructing a defense*

No member of society has a right to teach any doctrine contrary to what society holds to be true.

Samuel Johnson (1986)

Words are sacred. They deserve respect. If you get the right ones, in the right order, you can nudge the world a little.

Tom Stoppard (1998)

"Why Are We Reading This Book?"

In the beginning was the word and the word was good . . . or was it? So much depends upon who's reading the word. In the most recent unit I taught on sexuality (see Chapter 7), a student objected to the novel *Deliver Us From Evie*, which her group had chosen to discuss in lit circles. I think the book is an important one. It explores stereotypes, shows how sexuality affects family members, and offers gay students hope that they can handle discrimination and paint themselves a positive future. Kerri, however, complained—not to anyone in particular, but loud enough for me to hear—"Why are we reading this book? What's it got to do with English?"

I didn't answer her questions then but thought about them later. Kerri had become a favorite student of mine. The semester before I'd invited her and eleven of her peers to enter a writing contest at Miami University. Out of 150 participants, she was one of ten whose work was published. Besides being a good writer, Kerri's an asset to class discussion. She's insightful; she's thoughtful; she's respectful. Although my goal isn't to have my students like me, I think Kerri did like me, and I wanted to keep her on my good side.

Defending Texts

As I thought about her objections to the book (and to this unit on sexuality), I considered my teaching goals and asked myself, "What <u>does</u> *Deliver Us From Evie* have to do with teaching English?" To answer that question, I thought about other books I've taught over the years:

- *To Kill a Mockingbird*, which explores discrimination towards blacks
- *The Grapes of Wrath*, which explores discrimination towards migrants
- *Night*, which explores discrimination toward Jews

Students never objected to these books (at least not because of the racial, class, or religious discrimination they contain). So why had Kerri objected to a novel about discrimination toward gays?

I know Kerri is religious. She's said in class she's a Christian. Although her younger brothers continually get into trouble in and out of school, she says she was "baptized" several years ago. They have flunked out or dropped out, but she's at the top of her class. Although they were unpleasant and belligerent, she's cordial and cooperative. I can't imagine a teacher not welcoming Kerri into her class.

Coincidentally, Kerri returned to my classroom during my prep period. "Did I leave my purse in here, Mr. Gaughan?" she asked.

"I didn't see it, Kerri. Sorry," I replied.

"Thanks anyway."

"Kerri, before you go, may I talk to you?"

"Sure."

"I heard you wondering about the book you're reading in lit circles."

She lowered her eyes a split second, then raised them and said, "Yeah, I don't get why we're reading these books in an English class."

"We read books in here all the time. Kerri, What's your objection to this one?"

"I don't think we should talk about issues like this in school."

"Do you mean issues like discrimination? Last semester we read about Native Americans being discriminated against. How is this different?"

"I don't think we should talk about homosexuality in school. It says in the Bible that homosexuality's a sin, and I don't think we should talk about it."

So there it was. The *issue* that concerned Kerri wasn't discrimination, but sexuality. Homosexuality.

"Doesn't the Bible say we should love our neighbors as ourselves?" I asked her.

"I don't treat gay people different than I do anyone else, but being gay is a sin. God can judge them, not me."

I believed her. Kerri treats everyone equally. She's one of the nicest people in the school.

"I know you wouldn't treat anyone badly, but what about your peers? You've heard some of their comments, some of the words they use (fag, queer, lezzie). Don't you think books like *Evie* might make them rethink their attitudes?"

"I think their parents should talk to them about it, but not teachers in school. I've got to find my purse now, okay?"

"Okay, Kerri, I'll see you tomorrow."

I wanted Kerri to consider my words; I wanted her to say, "Yeah, you're right, Mr. Gaughan. I guess reading this book isn't any different than reading some of the other books we've read." But she didn't. She was polite; she listened; I'm not sure what she heard. What more could I say to her? What other reading might I ask her to do? How far could I push her thinking? Might I be overstepping my bounds?

The Bible and Homosexuality

Earlier that year Tom Romano had sent me a letter written by a friend addressing the Bible and homosexuality. I'd read it and stuffed it in a folder for this class. I reread it after my conversation with Kerri. Joe Pitkin had written an open letter to two men who objected to "medical benefits being extended to partners of homosexual employees" at New Mexico State University (Pitkin n.d.). Pitkin's letter addresses their objections. He proclaims himself Christian, as they do, but reminds them that Christians do not speak with a "unified voice on the issue of homosexuality." He points out that "even the most scrupulous fundamentalist Christian does not observe" certain things in the Bible, which was the basis of their argument. For example, Genesis "endorses polygamy, animal sacrifice, and levirate marriage (where, if a man dies without heirs, it is his brother's duty to have sex with the widow)," yet few, if any, people practice these customs today. He also mentions that eating shrimp or planting two kinds of seed in the same field was regarded as abominable, as is homosexuality in Leviticus 18:22. Yet no one today considers the first two practices abominations. Pitkin doesn't ask his readers to abandon the Bible but rather to "look to the spirit, which gives life, and not to the letter, which kills."

If that is a problem for readers, he asks them to suppose for the moment that homosexuality is a sin. Does it follow, he wonders, that gay partners of NMSU employees not receive benefits, especially considering that "sinful" heterosexual partners do receive them? "Might it not . . . be possible to offer benefits to the partners of gay employees not because their partners are gay but in spite of it?" When Tom e-mailed this article to me, he wrote that he found Pitkin's rhetoric powerful. I agreed.

"Too powerful?" I wondered later. On the one hand, I was compelled to read the piece aloud the next day in class. On the other, I doubted the wisdom of this. All year long I'd been asking students to reexamine their assumptions about gender, identity, war, and, now, homosexuality. The texts we'd read or watched provided lenses for them. In many cases those lenses proved catalysts for new thinking. Why this doubt about Pitkin's letter?

Considering Texts

When my students and I talk about identity or gender, race or war, they never base objections they have on the Bible. They usually revert to experience and observation (more commonly, parents' observations). With homosexuality, however, the Bible is almost exclusively the basis for their arguments. Many of these students who quote the Bible don't follow its other precepts, but with this issue, they fall back on what they believe the Bible says (most of them haven't actually read it). Pitkin has. He says that to his knowledge there are "three explicit references in the Bible to male homosexuality (there is not a word in the entire scripture which explicitly refers to lesbianism)." He's done his research and his argument is convincing.

Kerri isn't like the "many students" I mention above. She does read the Bible. In fact, a group of her and her friends meet before school every Friday with one of her other teachers to discuss what they've read. I respect that. It was Kerri and these friends who gave me pause. They weren't just using the Bible as a crutch to bash gays. They believed what they read.

Yes, the issue common to our study of race, class, gender, and homosexuality was discrimination, and on those grounds using Pitkin's piece struck me as legitimate. But that wasn't the only ground. Another was religious faith. Faith isn't logical, but Pitkin's argument is. I wondered about tampering with students' faith. Many experienced readers who believe homosexuality to be sinful might read Pitkin's letter and not have their faith shaken. They might agree with him that not paying benefits to partners of gay employees is discriminatory; yet they still could retain their faith. But could a sixteen- or seventeen-year-old do the same? Would this piece confuse Kerri, shake her faith, make her question the foundation that grounded her own behavior, especially in light of her brothers who constantly found themselves in trouble?

I shared Pitkin's piece with the teacher who led the Bible study group and agreed with her that I shouldn't use it. But still I wondered if I were censoring myself.

A week later I shared it with Tom Romano's English education students at Miami University. Most of them thought I'd made the wrong decision. One believed students need to question all aspects of their lives, even religious views. Another said the piece wasn't about faith, but about discrimination. "Use it," she said.

But a small minority thought differently. One wondered how parents of Kerri and her peers might respond. She thought I'd find myself on shaky ground, that she'd be upset with a teacher who gave such a piece to her child. Another young woman, who hadn't spoken the whole night, raised her hand at the end of class. Almost timidly, she admitted, "The student you're describing was me. I could not have handled this article if you'd given it to me in high school. I'm ready for it now. In fact, I constantly question my faith now that I'm in college."

I left Tom's class with mixed feelings. The majority of his students said they would have used Pitkin's letter. A few said they wouldn't. I was closer to my audience than they were. I'd considered the dilemma more than they had. I had eighteen more years teaching high school students than they did. But still, I wondered if I'd done the right thing.

Complicating Matters

As I drove home, the last comment from the young woman who said she was "my student" in high school resonated with me. Does age matter? I wouldn't give *The Diary of Anne Frank* to fourth-graders, as one of my wife's colleagues had. They're too young. I don't want my daughter to read *To Kill a Mockingbird* yet. She's in sixth grade. Teachers constantly consider maturity when they recommend texts for their students. Despite this line of reasoning, I couldn't shake the feeling that I was practicing self-censorship. Then I read part of a reflective letter by Laura Corbin, one of Tom's students, that she agreed to share with me. She confirmed what I just felt:

> This is the first piece of writing that I have felt compelled to write in a long time, perhaps the first piece that I have ever felt compelled to write. It is about the visit John Gaughan made to our classroom. I enjoyed his visit. . . . I learned much about thematic units . . . and how he decides which pieces to use. However, I was angered when we talked about the "Open Letter to Larry Sheffield and John Van Sweden." I was pissed off—sorry to use such strong language—but I was truly pissed off that he would not use this letter in his classroom. The reason made me even more upset: "It would shatter a student's beliefs." I feel that Mr. Gaughan is sheltering this student by not exposing her to other parts of the Bible, the parts that Joe Pitkin reveals to his readers.
>
> A reason for the sheltering was that she is not ready to hear about this subject quite yet. . . . My question is what if she never goes to college and is exposed to new ideas that may go against her view of her religion? Then her views will never change, and those views will be passed on to her children. I am sorry, but I do believe that this girl practices discrimination because she believes that gays are committing a sin. . . .
>
> I brought up my view in class, something I rarely do, but I raised my hand because I feel strongly about this subject, only to be told by another student that I was wrong. He said, "Christians accept the *person* but not the sin." That was the biggest load of BS I had heard all night. How can you accept the person but not their actions? I feel the actions make a person.
>
> I am a Christian and I attended a Bible study on Wednesday nights and Youth Group on Sunday nights in high school, and I can tell you for damn sure that we would have talked about this letter in respect to the Bible. We would have discussed that God does not judge, so neither should we. We would have related the Bible to present day topics because we are living in the present day, not 2000 years ago. Guess what else? There was a gay boy in that very same Youth Group. He didn't come out until after high school, where he was homecoming king, but what if he was in a church that didn't accept his homosexuality? How does Mr. Gaughan think the gay students out there feel when they have to hear the Bible thumpers (sorry) tell them that the Bible says he/she commits a sin, that he/she is immoral? I think homosexuals would be relieved to know that there is evidence in the Bible about other ridiculous sins, such as eating shrimp. Well, I guess I am just as bad as a gay person because I went to Olive Garden last night and had shrimp. Oh, and I think I was wearing clothing of two kinds of fibers, too. I must be going to hell.
>
> I think that this letter could be given as instruction to the students to let them know that views and beliefs can change. This letter

doesn't have to be a destroyer of faith, but a lesson that not everything the Bible says is true or right.

I feel the Bible needs to be interpreted from today's perspective, because times have changed. We amend the Constitution, don't we? . . . I feel that the Bible may need to be amended, also, because people have changed. What if they never would have amended the Constitution to let women vote? Just think about that. . . . We need to learn that with time, things change, eyes and minds are opened, and the door to faith never has to be closed.

Though the other young woman's comment struck me, this letter struck me harder. I was heartened that my visit and Pitkin's piece compelled her to write. That's what I hope all my teaching will do—compel students to speak. By speaking her mind, Laura made me rethink my position. What if Kerri didn't go to college? Would she ever encounter a piece like Pitkin's? Here was a student, Laura, who said she was Christian; she, like Kerri, had studied the Bible in high school, but her teacher would have had her students discuss this piece. Was I sheltering Kerri unnecessarily?

New Ideas

At the end of the sexuality unit, students wrote two- to three-page reflections. Kerri entitled hers "New Ideas":

Going into this unit I really didn't want to read *Deliver Us From Evie.* I love to read, but a novel about lesbians just didn't interest me. I still don't really like the book very much, but it did serve its purpose well. Through reading this novel . . . I was able to see the persecution homosexuals endure and the pain they suffer just because they are who they are. . . .

I have been raised by both my mother and by society knowing heterosexuality as normal . . . and homosexuality as abnormal. . . . I know this is awful to say, but I am being brutally honest here. I have always thought that gay couples somehow weren't real couples. It was always in my head that love and emotion just couldn't be part of a homosexual relationship, that gay relationships were simply compiled of confused and perverted sexual thrills. Until I read this novel, I had never seen a different side to this extremely controversial subject.

> I sat around watching TV, watching Evie sit around waiting
> for the phone to ring. I knew that was what she was doing.
> She kept looking at her watch, pacing, opening Cokes, and
> eating a lot of licorice candy. (Kerr 1994a, 111)

As soon as I read Parr's words in this quote, the thought hit me. It was perhaps the most important thought that entered my mind throughout the entire reading of the novel: perhaps the exact thought

Mr. Gaughan hoped would cross our minds while reading our books. I said to myself, "Hey, I've done that before." After that a whole train of thoughts bombarded my mind. "We've all done that. Every single person who has ever been in a relationship has done that at one point in time. That is just so normal. It's hard to believe Evie would do that. But is it? Maybe they really aren't *all* that different. Maybe."

I then went back and thought about all the parts of the novel that supported this crazy new idea. . . . I thought about the time when Patsy lied to her father and didn't tell Duff she was going to a concert with Evie. Neither one of the girls told their parents that Biker Pike was a lesbian band. I thought about how typical this was of any teenager. Not just heterosexual or homosexual teenagers, any teenagers. All the time I hear about kids lying to their parents about whom they're with or where they're going. I've done it myself plenty of times.

I thought about Evie making Patsy a valentine and how Evie would always wear the red scarf Patsy had bought for her. I thought about how no one could convince Evie to quit smoking except Patsy. All the pieces seemed to fit together . . .

However, my opinion still remains the same towards homosexuality. I still think it is wrong, disgusting, and perverted and I always will.

Though this final thought troubles me, I'm gratified that the book did "serve its purpose," as Kerri says. She does acknowledge what Mike in Chapter 7 did: that Evie and Patsy are *people* who love each other, that she has experienced what they have. Realizing what they have in common compels Kerri to reread parts of the novel to review them in light of this new understanding. Perhaps this is as far as she can move right now . . . perhaps not.

I wonder about the foundation of faith upon which Kerri grounds her life. How important is that faith to her? Could it withstand challenges that shake her foundation? I know that a single mother has raised her and her brothers. I know that her mother has been divorced twice, raised six children, and worked full-time at General Electric since graduating from high school. Kerri wonders in her journal how her mother stands "half of what she goes through—from cheating husbands, to cancer, to rotten kids, to financial struggles, the list is endless." Considering the familial instability Kerri has endured, I wonder if her religious faith is the only stability she has. If that is where she finds her solace?

Faith and Censorship

Recently, my sister-in-law Lisa passed away. She'd just turned forty. She died unexpectedly of an aneurysm. She was my wife's only sibling, my daughters' favorite aunt. The day Lisa died was difficult for all of us.

We each mourned in our own ways. Amy and Kelly eventually went to the computer and each typed Lisa a letter. They said how much they missed her, that they knew they'd see her again. In heaven. Their faith sustained them through the most difficult period in their young lives. Kelly is nine; Amy is twelve.

Kerri's sixteen. Maybe Pitkin's letter *would* move her further. But maybe it would shatter her faith, the only solid ground she may have to stand on right now. I don't know. I do know that Kerri's and Laura's and Pitkin's words moved me. They made me think about the Bible and homosexuality. They made me think about writing and teaching. They made me think about freedom and censorship. The student from Tom's class who said she'd be worried about parents' reactions to Pitkin's piece concerned me as it did her. I do consider the backlash other's words might stir. I weigh the texts I choose for the classroom in light of that—will provocative words do more than provoke students to think?

As I reconsider now the decision I made then about sharing Joe Pitkin's letter with Kerri, I think I was right. In that context. And context is everything. That's not to say I will never use his piece with future classes. But given Kerri's circumstances, I don't think it would've been right of me to challenge her faith. With other students, though, whose words spring from hate, not faith, I may share Pitkin's words for their consideration.

Constructing a Defense

I mustered a mental defense of these texts—just in case. The school mission statement is my first support:

> Lockland City Schools, in collaboration with the parents and community, educates and empowers each student to become a lifelong learner and a law-abiding, productive citizen in an ever-changing, diverse, global society.

The last words of this statement are important ones: our society *is* changing and it *is* diverse. I want all my students to see themselves mirrored in our school system. They need to read books about characters like themselves, by authors like themselves. That includes Jordan from Chapter 7, who's bisexual. Literature gives us a chance to try on someone else's shoes, to walk around in them for a while, to see what the world looks like through different eyes.

Kindred helps us understand what it was like to be black in the antebellum South; *The House on Mango Street*, what it's like growing up Hispanic in Chicago; *Annie on My Mind*, what it's like to fall in love and, at the same time, discover you're gay. Most of us in Lockland can never know these experiences personally, but through literature we can know, and school is about knowledge and knowing. If our district is sincere about its mission statement, then we must acknowledge diversity and appreciate it so we can live together *with* our differences in the twenty-first century.

9

Contact and Context

A Day After Watching Part One of *El Norte*

Terri: Mr. Gaughan, can I talk to you about this movie?

Mr. G.: Sure, Terri, what's up?

Terri: I wanted to know if I could get a makeup assignment. I don't think this is a good movie for school.

Mr. G.: What your problem with it, Terri?

Terri: I don't believe in watching movies with lots of cussing in them. It's against my religion.

Mr. G.: I know there's some cussing in Spanish, but you'll see tomorrow it helps Enrique get out of a jam.

Terri: Maybe, but I talked to Sister Feldon at church this morning, and she said it would be wrong for me to watch any more of the movie.

Mr. G.: It's okay with me if you do another assignment, Terri. How about responding to some of these articles about immigration?

Terri: Sure.

Mr. G.: I'll see if you can report to the library tomorrow, okay?

Terri: Okay. Thanks, Mr. Gaughan.

Mr. G: See you later, Terri.

Two days later, Terri transferred out of my English class.

Letter to Mr. Sheffield

Dear Mr. Sheffield:

Thank you for expressing your concerns about <u>The Drowning of Stephan Jones.</u> I'm sorry you feel as you do about the subject matter. Besides providing students with opportunities to read, write, and speak, I want them to explore real issues that interest and provoke them.

Throughout the semester I've asked students to consider difference: the plight of Native Americans in Sherman Alexi's "Amusements"; the humiliation of poverty in Dick Gregory's "Shame"; the discrimination gays face in <u>Stephan Jones.</u>

One goal of this course is examining other perspectives. I don't tell students what to think; I don't have that right. I do want them to recognize, though, that not everyone thinks as they do. They should be prepared to consider and respond to opinions and arguments different from their own.

I read recently that the city of Cincinnati lost more than 35 million dollars since the passage of Issue Three, which in essence permits discrimination based on sexuality. I mention this not to legitimize homosexuality, but to suggest that this issue is a legitimate one to explore in a class that deals with relevant contemporary issues.

You say in your letter that the Bible condemns homosexuality. The Bible also says people should love their neighbors as themselves. I'm not asking students to accept homosexuality as "right," but I am hoping they'll see discrimination as wrong.

I'm sorry you want Marcia removed from my class, but I understand your decision.

Thank you for bringing your concerns to my attention.

Sincerely,
John Gaughan

A Course Proposal

A friend in a neighboring district proposed a course similar to the Women and Men course I teach at Lockland. Katy wrote a vignette about her experience and presented it with three of her peers and me at the 1997 NCTE convention in Detroit in a session called, "Whose Morals Are We Talking About? Language in the Contact Zone." She calls the piece "Open Door . . . Open Mind?" alluding to the open-door policy a new superintendent set when he was first hired by the district. After proposing her course, she received a memo reading, "Upon review, Women in Literature course not approved for upcoming year."

Taking the superintendent at his word, she asked for a meeting. Her request was granted and, upon entering the room with her department head, she found four male administrators across the table from her. Katy opens the conversation by asking if the memo means she'll have to wait a year to begin the course. The superintendent replies, "No, Katy, we're not going to approve the course. I don't see any valid pedagogical reason for high school students to specialize so early in their academic careers."

Katy explains that after polling her students, forty-five of them expressed an interest in a women's lit elective, that she decided to propose the course in the first place because of a student request. Dr. B. responds that student interest wasn't an issue. He continues, "I just don't see any reasonable rationale behind allowing our students to narrow their focus so early."

Katy responds, "But there isn't time to really explore a single area of study in the regular curriculum. This elective is a great solution."

Dr. B. replies, "Then why women's literature?" and Katy thinks, *OK! You're finally out with it. . . .* "Frankly, it's because it is a personal interest of mine and . . ."

Dr. B.: A "personal interest"?

Katy: Well, yes—a specialty of sorts, you might say. *Oh, I get it—I'm 33 and single—he probably thinks I have some kind of lesbian agenda I'm trying to push or something.*

At the end of the meeting, Katy says, "So it's not a go," to which Dr. B. replies, "No."

"Not next year."

"Not ever."

* * *

Teaching in the contact zone is risky business. It may offend the sensibilities of students and parents, administrators and colleagues. Some teachers may not find these risks worth taking. It isn't pleasant to deal with challenges to our teaching. It would be much safer to keep ourselves and our students in our own and their comfort zones, never to enter the contact zone at all. By avoiding issues of race and gender, class and culture, sex and sexuality, we can spare ourselves the messy confrontations that revolve around religion and censorship, family values and school politics. But would we be sparing our students similar confrontations later?

Terri, who left my class two days after watching *El Norte* so she wouldn't have to face those issues herself, wrote a paper for a colleague of mine in which she discussed her dilemma. She said it was against her religion to watch R-rated movies and to read those kinds of words (the cussing she referred to was spoken in Spanish, subtitled in English). Her religion said she'd go to hell. My colleague, Linda Tatman, asked her if it was fair to judge a movie based on a few words, suggesting that that would be like judging a person by their appearance. She knew Terri planned on post-secondary education and wondered how she'd avoid similar dilemmas at the college level. "I'll just go somewhere where everyone thinks like I do."

Terri currently attends Ohio State.

I know that religious and family values are powerful forces in many of my students' lives. Avoiding hell is a powerful motivation for many students. I know that some of their parents would object to what I teach and how I teach it, but I know others would applaud what I do. So whose values do we promote?

Mr. Sheffield contacted the counselor and had his daughter Marcia removed from my class when he saw she was reading *The Drowning of Stephan Jones*. He didn't want her reading about homosexuality. His objections were based on religious grounds, just as Kerri's were in Chapter 8. I don't object to his objections, but I'd like to provide Marcia (and all my students) an opportunity to explore controversial issues and make up their own minds about them. If they decide, as Terri did, to transfer to another class, I'll respect their decision. The irony with Terri is that the year after she withdrew from my class, she approached me about taking an independent study course, saying she probably should have remained in my Contemporary Culture class the year before. "I heard it wasn't so bad after I left," she said. *It never was bad*, I thought, *but the senior "you" is different from the junior "you." You're probably ready for Ohio State now.*

Students have not raised most of the objections I've encountered since I began teaching in the contact zone. Usually parents, administrators, and board members object (though, luckily for me, objections have been relatively few). Parents object because they're truly offended; administrators and board members, because they're truly worried— worried that parents will be offended. I understand their concerns. They don't want to deal with challenges to the school's curriculum; they don't want to handle negative publicity (especially when school levies appear on the November ballot). But consider what they might have to deal with instead: sexual harassment, racial slurs, maybe even, as at Columbine, dead students.

I find it ironic that Mary Pierce Brosmer, who sparked my own curricular revolution, had to found her own school to do the kind of teaching my school permits me to do. That Katy, who proposed a course in gender studies, met with such administrative resistance in her district, whereas the course I proposed was accepted in mine. What are the men who resist such curricular changes afraid of? Maybe the answer lies in the writing of my students: when a young woman tells "herstory" as do Vicky and Kelly in Chapter 5, she might reveal a manipulative boyfriend, an abusive father, maybe even a savage rapist. Rather, keep the curriculum focused on "history" with its "litany of bloody dates" and "heroic" males who conquer, civilize, and protect. That "safe" story—safe at least as far as a traditional curriculum goes—may be perpetuating violence instead of confronting it.

I believe that education can save society. I have to believe that. I think immersing students in thematic contexts that address the issues I've discussed here, that encourage students to examine their language and to explore the assumptions that underlie their thinking, can save us. Using the ladder of prejudice (Chapter 5) as the framework for such a course might prove a good start. Travis, from that chapter, admitted, after taking Women and Men, that "sexism can kill." Jordan, after a semester of War and the Holocaust, came out of the closet. His friend Kristi didn't abandon him as Ronnie's "friend" did in "Right Off the Bat."

Through this book I relate a number of teaching strategies that have engaged my students and me. You and your students might find them engaging, too. But teaching strategies are not enough. Long-term, sustained thinking requires immersion. Consider the thematic contexts presented here and others that you and your students might invent. Don't just experiment with strategies. Create a context.

WORKS CITED

Alexie, S. 1993. "Amusements." In *The Lone Ranger and Tonto Fistfight in Heaven*, 54–58. New York: HarperCollins.

Amistad. 1997. Director: S. Spielberg. Dream Works. 152 min.

Ansen, D., and A. Samuels. 1997. "Amistad's Struggle." In *Newsweek* 130 (23): 64–67.

Arrick, F. 1981. *Chernowitz.* New York: Signet.

Barbieri, M. 1995. *Sounds from the Heart: Learning to Listen to Girls.* Portsmouth, N.H.: Heinemann.

Beach, R. 1995. "Stances of Resistance and Engagement in Responding to Multicultural Literature." Presentation, NCTE, San Diego.

Brosmer, M. P. 1983. "Mama." *With Fine Stitches,* unpublished manuscript, reprinted by permission of the author.

———. 1984. "history/herstory." *With Fine Stitches,* unpublished manuscript, reprinted by permission of the author.

Bunting, E. 1980. *Terrible Things: An Allegory of the Holocaust.* Philadelphia: The Jewish Publication Society.

Butler, O. 1979. *Kindred.* Boston: Beacon Press.

Carey-Webb, A. 1993. "Racism and Huckleberry Finn: Censorship, Dialogue, and Change." In *English Journal* 82 (7): 22–34.

Casualties of War. 1990. Director: B. De Palma. Westgate Video. 120 min.

Chase, G. 1990. "Perhaps We Just Need to Say Yes." *In Journal of Education* 172 (1): 29–37.

Cisneros, S. 1989. *The House on Mango Street.* New York: Vintage.

Cole, P. 1996. "Where Have All the Cowboys Gone?" On *This Fire,* WEA/ Warner Brothers.

Come See the Paradise. 1991. Director: A. Parker. Twentieth Century Fox. 135 min.

Creekbaum, M. 2000. "Pearl Levy/Katherine Millard." In *Blending Genre, Altering Style,* T. Romano, 104–106. Portsmouth, N.H.: Heineman.

Cullen, C. 1997. "Incident." In *The Norton Anthology of Poetry,* ed. M. Ferguson, M. Salter, and J. Stallworthy, 833. New York: W. W. Norton and Company.

Cunningham, L. 1995. "Business As Usual." In *Writing With Passion: Life Stories, Multiple Genres,* T. Romano: 179–81. Portsmouth, N.H.: Heinemann.

Daniels, H., and M. Bizar. 1998. *Methods That Matter: Six Structures for Best Practice Classrooms*. York, Maine: Stenhouse Publishers.

Disclosure. 1994. Director: B. Levinson. Warner Studios. 129 min.

El Norte. 1983. Director: G. Nava. Cinecom International Films. 141 min.

Ellison, R. 1964. "Change the Joke and Slip the Yoke." *Shadow and Act*, 61–73. New York: Signet.

The Fairer Sex. 1993. On *Prime Time Live*. New York: ABC News. 16 min.

Falling Down. 1993. Director: J. Schumacher. Warner Studios. 113 min.

Fleischman, P. 1985. *I Am Phoenix: Poems For Two Voices*. New York: Harper & Row.

Forester, E. M. 1986. In *Writers on Writing*, ed. J. Winokur, 20. Philadelphia: Running Press.

Garden, N. 1982. *Annie on My Mind*. New York: Farrar, Straus and Giroux.

Gardner, S. 1997. "Life in Gangland." In *Identity: Who We Are*, ed. L. Gardner and M. Rinn, 28–33. Mahwah, N.J.: Troll Communications.

Gaughan, J. 1997. *Cultural Reflections: Critical Teaching and Learning in the English Classroom*. Portsmouth, NH: Boynton-Cook.

Gentry, C. 1990. "Stereotypes of Women Are Alive and Well." *The Chicago Tribune*, A–11, 18 August.

Gilligan, C. 1982. *In a Different Voice*. Cambridge, Mass.: Harvard University Press.

Gilman, C. P. 1985. "The Yellow Wall-Paper." In *Literature: Options for Reading and Writing*, ed. D. Daiker, M. Fuller, and J. Wallace, 117–131. New York: Harper & Row.

Giroux, H. A. 1992. *Border Crossings: Cultural Workers and the Politics of Education*. New York: Routledge.

Glaspell, S. 1985. "A Jury of Her Peers." In *Literature: Options for Reading and Writing*, ed. D. Daiker, M. Fuller, and J. Wallace, 13–31. New York: Harper & Row.

Goldberg, N. 1986. *Writing Down the Bones*. Boston: Shambhala.

Gore, L. 1963a. "It's My Party." On *The Golden Hits of Lesley Gore*, Mercury Records.

———. 1963b. "Judy's Turn to Cry." On *The Golden Hits of Lesley Gore*, Mercury Records.

Graves, D. 1983. *Writing: Teachers and Children at Work*. Portsmouth, N.H.: Heinemann.

Gregory, D. 1990. "Shame." *In Emerging Voices: A Cross-Cultural Reader*, ed. J. Madden-Simpson and S. Blake, 285–288. Ft. Worth, Tex.: Holt, Rinehart, Winston.

Greene, B. 1991. *The Drowning of Stephan Jones*. New York: Bantam Books.

Greene, M. 1995. *Releasing the Imagination: Essays on Education, the Arts, and Social Change*. San Francisco: Jossey-Bass Publishers.

Harris, J. 1995. "Negotiating the Contact Zone." In *Journal of Basic Writing* 14 (1): 27–42.

Heimel, C. 1996. "Diary of a Single Mother." In *From Community to School: Reading and Writing Across Diverse Contexts*, ed. J. Sommers and C. Lewiecki-Wilson, 46–51. New York: St. Martin's Press.

Hynds, S. 1997. *On The Brink: Negotiating Literature and Life with Adolescents.* New York: Teachers College Press.

Ingraham, P. 1997. *Creating and Managing Learning Centers: A Thematic Approach.* Peterborough, N.H.: Crystal Springs Books.

Johnson, S. 1986. In *Writers on Writing*, ed. J. Winokur, 148. Philadelphia: Running Press.

Jones, A., and L. Newman. 1997. *Our America: Life and Death on the South Side of Chicago.* New York: Washington Square Press.

Josefowitz, N. 1983. "Impressions from an Office." In *Is This Where I Was Going?*, 6–7. New York: Warner Books.

Kerr, M. E. 1994a. *Deliver Us From Evie.* New York: HarperCollins.

———. 1994b. "We Might As Well All Be Strangers." In *Am I Blue? Coming Out from the Silence*, ed. M. Bauer, 19–27. New York: HarperCollins.

Kincaid, J. 1983. "Girl." In *Experiencing Race, Class, and Gender in the United States*, ed. V. Cyrus, 70–71. Mountain View, Calif.: Mayfield Publishing Company.

King, M. L. 1963. "Letter from the Birmingham Jail." In *Atlantic Monthly* 212 (2): 78–88.

Kingsolver, B. 1989. "Rose-Johnny." In *Homeland and Other Stories*, 203–225. New York: HarperCollins.

———. 1995. "The Spaces Between." In *High Tide in Tuscon: Essays from Now or Never*, 146–157.

Kinsella, W. P. 1978. "Black Wampum." In *Scars*, 102–111. Canada, Oberon.

———. 1986. "Lark Song." In *Dance Me Outside*, 114–120. Boston: David R. Codine, Inc.

Kolbenschlag, M. 1979. *Kiss Sleeping Beauty Good-Bye.* San Francisco: Harper and Row.

Lame Deer, J., and R. Erdoes. 1972. "Talking to the Owls and Butterflies." In *Lame Deer: Seeker of Visions*, 119–141. New York: Washington Square Press.

Lasky, K. 1996. "To Stingo With Love: An Author's Perspective on Writing Outside One's Culture." *The New Advocate* 9 (1): 1–7.

Lee, H. 1960. *To Kill a Mockingbird.* New York: Popular Library.

Lifshin, L. 1978. *Tangled Vines: A Collection of Mother and Daughter Poems.* Boston: Beacon Press.

Maher, F. 1985. "Women Students in the Classroom." In *Rereading America: Cultural Contexts for Critical Thinking and Writing*, ed. G. Colombo, R. Cullen, and B. Lisle, 493–503. New York: St. Martin's.

Marklein, M. 1990. "Learning to Give Girls Equal Classroom Attention." In *Experiencing Race, Class, and Gender in the United States,* ed. V. Cyrus, 242–43. Mountain View, Calif.: Mayfield Publishing Company.

McCourt, F. 1999. *'Tis: A Memoir.* New York: Scribner.

Mead, M. 1996. *The New Beacon Book of Quotations by Women,* ed. R. Maggio, 7. Boston: Beacon Press.

Meyette, T. 1988. "Trading Post—Winslow, Arizona." In *A Gathering of Spirit: A Collection By North American Indian Women,* ed. B. Bryant, 42. New York: Firebrand Books.

Miller, R. 1994. "Fault Lines in the Contact Zone." *College English* 56 (4): 389–408.

Miner, H. 1956. "The Body Ritual Among the Nacirema." *American Anthropologist* 58 (3): 503–507.

Nelms, B. 1994. "Reinventing English." *English Journal* 82 (3): 104–05.

Newman, L. 1999. "Right Off the Bat." In *Identity Lessons: Contemporary Writing About Learning to Be American,* ed. M. Gillan and J. Gillan, 120–26. New York: Penguin.

Nightjohn. 1996. Director: C. Burnett. Hallmark Home Entertainment. 96 min.

Noddings, N. 1992. *The Challenge to Care in Schools: An Alternative Approach to Education.* New York: Teachers College Press.

Obedience. 1969. Milgram, S. Yale University. 45 min.

Ogden, M. 1989. "Hangman." In *The Holocaust: Prejudice Unleashed,* ed. L. Rabinsky and C. Danks, Chapter 2, 4–5. Ohio Council on Holocaust Education.

Orkin, R. 1951. "American Girl in Italy." In *Ruth Orkin Photo Archive,* orkin .photo.com/amergirl.

Parker, D. 1976. "The Sexes." In *The Portable Dorothy Parker,* 24–28. New York: Penguin.

Parker, J. G. 1989. "What Is Poverty?" In *Model Voices: Finding a Writing Voice,* ed. J. Sommers, 148–53. New York: McGraw-Hill.

Paulsen, G. 1993. *Nightjohn.* New York: Delacorte.

Perrotta, T. 1994. "Forgiveness." In *Bad Haircut.* New York: Berkley.

Pirie, B. 1997. *Reshaping High School English.* Urbana, Ill.: NCTE.

Pitkin, J. n.d. "An Open Letter." Unpublished letter, excerpts reprinted by permission of the author.

The Power of One. 1992. Director: J. Avildsen. Warner Studios. 127 min.

Pratt, M. L. 1991. "Arts of the Contact Zone." *Profession* 91. New York: MLA: 33–40.

Pugh, S., J. Hicks, M. Davis, T. Venstra. 1992. *Bridging: A Teacher's Guide to Metaphorical Thinking.* Urbana, Ill.: NCTE.

Quindlen, A. 1994. "Society's Curious Math Devalues Women's Lives." *The Cincinnati Enquirer,* E–3, 30 October.

Rochlin, M. 1992. "The Heterosexual Questionnaire." In *Men's Lives,* ed. M. Kimmel and M. Messner, 482–83. New York: Macmillan Publishing Company.

Romano, T. 2000. *Blending Genre, Altering Style.* Portsmouth, N.H.: Heinemann.

Salinger, J. D. 1951. *The Catcher in the Rye.* Boston: Little, Brown and Company.

Sandburg, C. 1985. "Chicago." In *The Norton Anthology of American Literature,* ed. N. Baym et al., 1065–1066. New York: W. W. Norton and Company.

Santayana, G. 1980. In *Bartlett's Familiar Quotations,* ed. E. Beck, 703. Boston: Little, Brown and Company.

Seto, T. 1995. "Multiculturalism Is Not Halloween." *The Horn Book* 71 (2): 169–74.

Seven Mary Three. 1995. "Water's Edge." On *American Standard,* Carrboro, N.C.: Mammoth Records.

Sommers, N. 1984. "Revision Strategies of Student Writers and Experienced Adult Writers." In *Rhetoric and Composition: A Sourcebook for Teachers and Writers,* ed. R. Graves, 328–337. Portsmouth, N.H.: Boynton/Cook.

Spiegelman, A. 1986. *Maus I: A Survivor's Tale: My Father Bleeds History.* New York: Pantheon.

Spiegelman, A. 1991. *Maus II: A Survivor's Tale: And Here My Troubles Began.* New York: Pantheon.

Stagecoach. 1939. Director: J. Ford. Warner Studios. 96 min.

Steinbeck, J. 1976. *The Grapes of Wrath.* New York: Penguin.

———. 1985. "The Murder." In *Literature: Options for Reading and Writing,* ed. D. Daiker, M. Fuller, and J. Wallace, 13–31. New York: Harper & Row.

Strasser, T. 1981. *The Wave.* New York: Dell.

Stoppard, T. 1998. Quoted in an exhibition at the Freedom Forum, Washington, D.C.

Syfers, J. 1993. "I Want a Wife." In *Experiencing Race, Class, and Gender in the United States,* ed. V. Cyrus, 75–77. Mountain View, Calif.: Mayfield.

Thomas, A. 1991. *Life in the Ghetto.* Kansas City, Mo.: Landmark Editions, Inc.

Thompson, J. 1993. "Helping Students Control Texts: Contemporary Literary Theory into Classroom Practice." In *Constructive Reading: Teaching Beyond Communication,* ed. S. Straw and D. Bodgan. Portsmouth, N.H.: Boynton/Cook.

Townsend, P. 1983. "Who Are You?" On *The Who's Greatest Hits,* Universal City, CA: MCA Records.

Triumph of the Spirit. 1990. Director: R. Young. Polygram Video. 120 min.

Twain, M. 1984. *The Adventures of Huckleberry Finn.* New York: Signet.

Vaughan, K., and N. Clarke. 1999. "Note Blames the Victims." *RockyMountain News.com,* 19 April.

Walker, A. 1982. *The Color Purple.* New York: Washington Square Press.

War and Remembrance. 1988. Director: D. Curtis. MPI Home Video. 840 min.

The West, Vol. 9: One Sky Above Us. 1996. Director: K. Burns. PBS Home Video. 62 min.

Wiesel, E. 1960. *Night.* New York: Bantam.

Witness. 1985. In *Understanding the Film: An Introduction to Film Appreciation,* 49. Lincolnwood, Ill.: National Textbook Company.

Wolff, J. M. 1996. "Teaching in the Contact Zone: The Myth of Safe Houses." *Critical Theory and the Teaching of Literature: Politics, Curriculum, Pedagogy.* NCTE: Urbana, Ill.: 316–327.

Woodard, F., and D. MacCann. 1992. "Minstrel Shackles and Nineteenth-Century 'Liberality' in *Huckleberry Finn.*" In *Satire or Evasion? Black Perspectives on Huckleberry Finn,* ed. J. Leonard, T. Tenney, and T. Davis, 141–153. Durham: Duke UP.

Yamada, M. 1994. "Cincinnati." In *Unsettling America: An Anthology of Contemporary Multicultural Poetry,* ed. M. M. Gillan and J. Gillan, 79–80. New York: Penguin.

Yolen, J. 1994. "An Empress of Thieves." *The Horn Book,* 70 (6): 702–705.